Daniel in Babylon

Daniel in Babylon

How He Navigated Politics in Exile
and What It Means for Us Today

MARK T. CLARK

Foreword by Hugh Ross

WIPF & STOCK · Eugene, Oregon

DANIEL IN BABYLON
How He Navigated Politics in Exile and What It Means for Us Today

Copyright © 2025 Mark T. Clark. All rights reserved. Except for brief quotations in critical publications or reviews, no part of this book may be reproduced in any manner without prior written permission from the publisher. Write: Permissions, Wipf and Stock Publishers, 199 W. 8th Ave., Suite 3, Eugene, OR 97401.

Wipf & Stock
An Imprint of Wipf and Stock Publishers
199 W. 8th Ave., Suite 3
Eugene, OR 97401

www.wipfandstock.com

PAPERBACK ISBN: 979-8-3852-3111-9
HARDCOVER ISBN: 979-8-3852-3112-6
EBOOK ISBN: 979-8-3852-3113-3

01/31/25

All Scripture quotations, unless otherwise indicated, are taken from the Holy Bible, New International Version®. NIV®. Copyright©1973, 1978, 1984, 2011 by Biblica, Inc.™ Used by permission of Zondervan. All rights reserved worldwide. www.zondervan.com The "NIV" and "New International Version" are trademarks registered in the United States Patent and Trademark Office by Biblica, Inc.™

This book is dedicated to those who understand—or would like to understand more fully—what it means to have dual citizenship, first in the kingdom of Heaven and second in our native country, to know how to live as exiles in the land.

"It is too small a thing for you to be my servant, to restore the tribes of Jacob and bring back those of Israel I have kept. I will also make you a light for the Gentiles, that my salvation may reach to the ends of the earth."

ISAIAH 49:6

"This is what the Lord Almighty, the God of Israel, says to all those I carried into exile from Jerusalem to Babylon: '... Seek the peace and prosperity of the city to which I have carried you into exile. Pray to the Lord for it, because if it prospers, you too will prosper.'"

JEREMIAH 29:4–7

Contents

Lists of Illustrations and Tables	ix
Foreword by Hugh Ross	xi
Preface	xv
Acknowledgments	xvii
1 Introduction	1
2 Methodology: Abductive Reasoning	7
3 God's Sovereign Rule with Daniel in Babylon	18
4 Daniel's First Appeal: More Vegetables	42
5 Daniel's Second Appeal: More Time	58
6 Daniel's Third Appeal: A Non-Appeal with Appeal	76
7 Daniel's Fourth Appeal: For a Return to the Land	92
8 Daniel's Fifth Appeal: More Information	109
9 Assessing the Reliability of the Book of Daniel	124
Appendix A: Analysis of Competing Hypotheses	141
Appendix B: Key Assumptions Check	148
Appendix C: Intelligence Failure	151
Bibliography	153
Index	157

Lists of Illustrations and Tables

Table 1: Man Lying in a Gutter	10
Table 2: Sample Analyses of Competing Hypotheses	14
Table 3: Names	43
Table 4: Overlap of Daniel 1–2	59
Table 5: Dreams and Visions of Empires in Daniel	72
Table 6: Size of Four Empires of Daniel	72
Table 7: Kings of Babylon	77
Table 8: Visions and Timelines of Daniel	82
Table 9: Two Little Horns of Daniel	114
Table 10: Chiasm in Daniel 2–7	132
Table 11: Probabilities Within a "Fuzzy" System	139
Table 12: Analysis of Competing Hypotheses (ACH)	141
Table 13: Key Assumptions Check	150
Figure 1: Levels of God's Sovereign Rule	30

Foreword

YEARS AGO, I DEBATED Tim Callahan, religion editor for *Skeptic*, on this question: Does the Bible have predictive power? Tim argued that there are no verifiable predictions of future events or scientific discoveries in the Bible. He claimed there is nothing supernatural about the Bible, no basis for an educated person to conclude that it is divinely inspired. I argued that the Bible frequently predicts specific events and anticipates scientific discoveries that the authors could not have "guessed."

Much of our debate focused on the book of Daniel. Callahan claimed that the significant political events depicted as Daniel's "visions" are later writings attributed to Daniel. He said that no one in the sixth century BC court of Babylon or the subsequent Medo-Persian court could have written the book of Daniel. Callahan asserted that the book was likely written in the second century BC, long after the events described had already occurred, with no "prophecy" involved.

To support this assertion, Callahan commented that the Greek musical instruments mentioned in Daniel's book were not commonly used in Babylon until a few centuries after the fall of Babylon. I countered by citing evidence that while not *all* Greek musical instruments were present in Babylon at the height of the empire, the three mentioned by Daniel were. I also pointed out that portions of the book of Daniel were discovered among the Dead Sea Scrolls, dated (by carbon-14) to the second century BC. What's more, the entirety of the book of Daniel is included in the Septuagint, the second-century BC Greek translation of the Old Testament. Today, no reputable history scholar disputes this early date for the Septuagint.

Given that multiple copies of the book of Daniel had been distributed throughout the Mediterranean and Middle Eastern region by (or before) the second century BC, insufficient time would have passed to deceive scholars and the general public into thinking that Daniel was composed in the sixth century BC. Daniel was widely known and revered among scholars and the general public throughout the region, where he had served as prime minister for both the Babylonian Empire and the Medo-Persian Empire. These people would not have been easily fooled by an imposter writing a few centuries later in Daniel's name. The historical evidence that the book of Daniel was written by the exile who rose to such heights of power seems especially strong.

Tim Callahan's denial of the Bible's predictive power was no surprise. He is an atheist/agnostic, after all. What shocked me, however, as I prepared for this debate, was I found that many Christian scholars of our time, including conservative evangelical Christian scholars, are reluctant to uphold the Bible's power to accurately predict future events in human history and future discoveries in science.

Soon after that debate, I began to see more and more articles and books by Christian scholars denying the Bible's predictive power. *The Lost World of Genesis One* by John Walton, a Wheaton College professor of theology and biblical archeology, challenged the long-held understanding of Gen 1 as a creation chronology. According to his view, the text refers to the "function" of God's creation activity, not the creative acts themselves or the order of those acts. He argued that it was a mistake to interpret Genesis as presenting a chronological narrative of God's action as Creator. Walton and, later, his coauthors claimed the Bible writers described only what they and their contemporaries believed about the world—its history and the realm of nature.

At the time, I was concerned that denying Genesis as an orderly and scientifically correct overview of creation would lead to denying the Bible's power to predict or anticipate anything in nature or history. Soon, my concern was realized. In 2013, Walton and Brent Sandy published *The Lost World of Scripture*, declaring that the prophecies in the Old Testament may not be predictive at all. They argued that the prophecies written in Daniel, Isaiah, and other Old Testament books had been written by the prophets and their students. They asserted that, for example, the books of Daniel and Isaiah should be understood as the writings of the prophetic "schools" they had established. These schools continued long after their lifetime. In other words, the "prophecies" in Daniel and Isaiah had most likely been written generations following their deaths—long after the prophesied events had occurred. Callahan, Walton, and Sandy seem to hold that the Old Testament lacks predictive power.

FOREWORD

While I have written a few words to defend the Bible's power to predict future events in human history, I have hoped and prayed for other scholars with appropriate background and insight to develop well-researched resources that could help turn the tide back toward trust in the supernatural revelation of Scripture. These resources must also make a solid case for God's behind-the-scenes involvement in human history and politics. Consequently, I was thrilled to learn that my good friend Mark Clark, a professor of political science specializing in international politics and intelligence studies, was writing a book on Daniel. This book could help believers and nonbelievers trust in the prophecies of Scripture and respond wisely to today's political crises.

Mark and I agree that the spiritual realm has always influenced politics and international affairs. History reflects illogical, irrational, and self-destructive decisions and miraculous outcomes that cannot be explained by human factors alone. There must be supernatural components. These components are explicitly identified in Dan 10:12–13 and 20–21 and further demonstrated in the whole of Dan 10–12. As the apostle Paul reminds us in Eph 6:11–13, "Put on the full armor of God, so that you can take your stand against the devil's schemes. For our struggle is not against flesh and blood, but against the rulers, against the authorities, against the powers of this dark world and against the spiritual forces of evil in the heavenly realms. Therefore put on the full armor of God, so that when the day of evil comes, you may be able to stand your ground, and after you have done everything, to stand."

There is a spiritual battle being waged in human politics. It involves all of us in one way or another. Daniel fought it more expertly, wisely, and graciously than any other human before or after him. We need to learn from Daniel how best to fight the good fight.

In this book, Mark shows how Daniel waged one battle after another, political and spiritual, with utmost integrity, relying on godly discernment to craft carefully thought out and carefully executed appeals, each distinct from the others, to those in power. To this day, Daniel's response to the most intense political and personal crises stands as an essential example of how to successfully serve God's purposes and follow his ways during crucial tests and challenges.

Mark explains that Daniel's successes were built on a lifetime of spiritual preparation. Mark shows readers how to emulate Daniel's humble yet confident faith when facing our political and personal dilemmas. I pray

FOREWORD

that readers of this book will also experience beneficial breakthroughs amidst colliding worldviews and values. In so doing, I pray that like Daniel we will become, in the eyes of the Lord, "highly esteemed" (Dan 9:23, 10:11, 19).

> Hugh Ross, PhD
> Founder and Senior Scholar, Reasons to Believe

Preface

LEON TROTSKY REPORTEDLY SAID, "You may not be interested in war, but war is interested in you."[1] What's true of war is even more true of politics and all things political. Wars come and go, but politics will remain with us until the end of the ages. This fact of our existence begs the question, How may we live wisely in all things political? That question has led to many books on philosophy, politics, and ethics, most of which are too remote for the average person to absorb. I should know. My field has been international relations, national security, and politics for over three decades.

Early in my academic career, I found a great practical resource that challenged my assumptions about living politically. That resource was the book of Daniel. Here was a young man, a boy likely, who was taken from his homeland and forced into exile, away from his family, his traditions, his culture, and his community of fellow Jews. Yet he rose to prominence over the course of two empires, the Babylonian and Persian. He navigated the politics of exile brilliantly and with humility and wisdom. He never seemed to desire revenge for the life he did not choose or the country to which he did not belong. In his obedience and humility, Daniel exemplifies what it means to live well with dual citizenship, the first in the kingdom of heaven and the second here on earth. Daniel speaks to us today and has spoken to countless others over the millennia. I hope you take as much encouragement and wisdom from this study as I did.

---

1. Wikipedia, "Leon Trotsky," see sec. "Attributed."

Acknowledgments

THERE ARE ALWAYS MANY people who deserve credit for any book. While it is a solitary endeavor, many people impact your research, writing, and teaching. First, I would like to thank Hugh Ross for proposing I teach his course Paradoxes early in the 1990s and that I focus it on how Daniel lived well politically. It was about the time when I was still an untenured assistant professor of a graduate program in National Security Studies. Neither the graduate program nor my public identification as an evangelical Christian was especially appreciated in the secular university. Teaching this study over six weeks or more in that class was more rewarding than I imagined. Over two hundred strong, the class consisted of scientists, engineers, and other professionals who asked great questions, challenged unstated assumptions, and provided substantive feedback. The study of Daniel helped me to learn to live well in an unfriendly environment.

I have taught this class in many church settings over many years. I have taught weeks-long Bible studies and given short one-hour presentations from the pulpit, in webinars, and in Zoom meetings. I've been interviewed on podcasts. I have spoken about Daniel and his approach to politics to youth groups, young adult groups, and adult lay and educated audiences in the Christian community. I am grateful to all the study participants. It has always been well received, especially during election seasons or when the political chaos of our nation was at the forefront for different reasons. Almost invariably, the response has been the same: the study of Daniel and how he lived elevated peoples' views of God's sovereign actions in history, including political history. I began to desire to put pen to paper when I "retired" from my academic career, and this book is the result.

Several people deserve some mention. They are all personal friends. First, I want to thank Krista Briley for helping me make the manuscript more accessible to a nontechnical audience. Second, Kathy Ross took the

ACKNOWLEDGMENTS

time to critique my assessment of how Daniel may have avoided the trauma of captivity. Editors like to edit, as she says, and she does it well. Third, I thank Carolyn McDonald, whose support for this project and joy in the face of many health challenges remind me that Daniels exists in many different ways. Fourth, Joshua Johnson, a senior intelligence analyst in the Defense Intelligence Enterprise, provided great feedback on the final chapter involving particular intelligence analysis techniques. Last, another friend, who needs to remain anonymous, reviewed several crucial chapters, including the final one. While I had multiple grants from the intelligence community, including one from the Intelligence Advanced Research Projects Activity to learn and teach intelligence analysis, nothing made the work more accurate and personal than the feedback of two senior intelligence analysts who continue to serve in the defense of our country.

I also want to thank my wife, Mara, for her patient endurance while I wrote this book. She gave me many resources that helped me to understand how trauma affects us and how it could have affected people like Daniel and his three friends. But, in some ways, she sacrificed even more than I did. During summers in Colorado, she would "give me time" to write by going out to fly fish in our local rivers on her own, with only our trusted pup, Caddis, for companionship. Only when she returned from her day trips to regale me with stories of large rainbows and browns did I feel she might have had the better deal, especially when those trout measured in at eighteen inches or more on a double-aught weight fly rod. To God be the glory, and to Mara, the fish!

1

Introduction

WHY ANOTHER BOOK ON Daniel? Many people have written books and monographs on the biblical book of Daniel. In my review of many of these works, I find at least seven different types of books that treat the subjects of Daniel's life, dreams, visions, prophecies, and the authenticity of his work. These seven types tend to be written from one or the other of two distinct philosophical assumptions: either (a) spiritual matters are real and trustworthy, or (b) such things are mythical or unreal. The perspectives of the vast majority of people throughout history have fallen into the first category, and only in the last several hundred years have many Western people adopted the latter view. As this view predominates in academia, it percolates throughout our society, particularly in the West, and spreads to the rest of the world.

Those who believe that spiritual matters are real include many pastors and theologians who have commented on the book of Daniel, with their commentary arising from their particular theological tradition. This group also includes authors who provide expository Bible studies that explore the life of Daniel and his faithfulness in Babylon.[1] Daniel is also the subject of a wide array of children's books, especially ones that focus on his courageous faith, either in the lion's den or when his three friends, Shadrach, Meshach, and Abednego, were in the fiery furnace. Then there are those authors who focus on the eschatology of the book of Daniel concerning the "end times," as Daniel employs more apocalyptic passages than any other book of the Old Testament. Finally, a fifth type of work includes writings from authors

1. See, for example, Hodges, *Daniel Dilemma*, Hood, *Daniel*, and Moore, *Lives*.

who defend the reliability of the book of Daniel.[2] The vast majority of these authors believe in the reliability and trustworthiness of Daniel based on the Christian (and Jewish) ideas of the inspiration and canonicity of Scriptures. These concepts assert that God inspired the work and retains the accuracy of what it records.

From the second category of those who discount spiritual matters are many authors who, from different perspectives, dispute the authenticity and reliability of the book of Daniel. These include those authors who assume a philosophical worldview of naturalism. Naturalists, in general, tend to believe that only those things that we can prove physically are reliable and trustworthy. They are mainly secular scholars, though some liberal theologians and non-scholars also find themselves in this group. Many, though not all, believe the book of Daniel to be a work of historical fiction, while others believe that some parts are fiction and others may be factual. I find it necessary to note here that some good secular scholars may adhere to this philosophy but betray no dismissiveness or condescension to the biblical record and provide good insight into the ancient world of Daniel.[3]

A newer group of writers on Daniel hold to a postmodernist approach. Postmodernism is a late twentieth-century philosophical school of thought that generally rejects the modern approaches to reason and science that have emerged since the Enlightenment. While there are many types of postmodernism, the *Encyclopedia Britannica* characterizes it well: postmodernists are skeptical, subjective, suspicious of reason, and acutely sensitive to the role of ideology in maintaining political and economic power.[4] These writers doubt the idea of truth and, in their literary criticism, typically believe that questions of authorship are unimportant. They tend to treat biblical stories as mere stories, not factual accounts that reflect authentic experiences from history or prophecy.[5] They regard such stories as interesting for the different communities that read and use them in their cultures at different times throughout history. To many in this school of thought, it is not the author but the audience that is important.

---

2. The classic defense is McDowell's *Critics' Den*.

3. Two scholars that give invaluable historical and archaeological insight without condescension to people of faith are Oates, *Babylon*, and Seymour, *Babylon*.

4. Duignan, "Postmodernism."

5. A good example of this genre is Fewell's *Circle*, where the author treats Daniel as a work of historical fiction yet has some intriguing insights.

INTRODUCTION

I look at and evaluate the book of Daniel in this manuscript differently. I use abductive reasoning to assess the book, both generally as to its reliability and specifically to flesh out the many nuances of what it records the author doing and saying. Abductive reasoning means reasoning to the best hypothesis or explanation, and it will be employed in this work to help the modern reader understand several things about the book of Daniel. Later in the book, I will use a particular form of abductive reasoning to determine whether the book of Daniel can be considered reliable and credible. In other words, does the book of Daniel pass the "smell" test? Did an authentic and credible human named Daniel, who lived in Babylon in the sixth century BC, write the book based on historical events? Does the book offer credible testimony to some incredible events and prophecies recorded in Babylon? Or did an anonymous Jew write it during the second century BC? Is it, therefore, a work of historical fiction? These are essential questions as the book has come under significant attack not only since the Enlightenment but particularly since the nineteenth century.

I also use abductive reasoning to explain many of the nuances of the book of Daniel. For example, I explain why Daniel may have chosen to request or appeal for a restrictive diet of vegetables in Dan 1 and why he didn't resist the pagan name of Belteshazzar given to him by court officials. I also reason to the best hypothesis for how Daniel may have avoided the trauma of forced captivity, a trauma that many people have suffered throughout history. Or, better yet, I reason how God may have helped Daniel avoid the trauma of forced captivity. I also use abductive reasoning to help us understand how Daniel made such wise appeals throughout his career, crafting remarkably mature approaches to situations without clearly defined solutions. I will also examine how Daniel employed the ancient biblical virtue of wisdom, a skill he used to seek balanced and respectful solutions to specific problems and dilemmas without black-and-white answers.

Daniel offers many exceptional examples of living wisely in tumultuous political times. Though our era differs from his, the problem of politics remains the same, and lessons from his life can help address questions such as, How shall we live and engage both our neighbors and our governing authorities in the realm of politics? How may we, like Daniel, maintain our witness in the realm of politics in our time?

The underlying principles of political communities rest on something fundamentally different than what the principles of Christian and Jewish communities rest upon. In the former, the physics of politics rests upon brute force and must always be evaluated through power relationships—ruler and ruled. To quote Thucydides, author of *The History of the Peloponnesian War*, in the politics of power "the strong do what they can and the weak suffer what they must."[6] On the other hand, the spiritual physics of God's kingdom rests on grace, respect for others, prayer, agape, or divine love. It finds its expression through the body of Christ, the church. We will examine how Daniel models engagement in politics while living for God's kingdom purposes. He demonstrates a way of living in the political realm of Babylonian and Persian politics while serving God's kingdom first and foremost.

The power relationship of politics may be a necessary concession to the human problem of sin. Since the fall, humans have repeatedly betrayed God's best purposes for themselves, for one another, and for the world itself. From early in Genesis, we see murder and evil so thoroughly rampant that God destroys the vast majority of humans through the flood and institutes capital punishment after it to restrain the evil of murder. Yet, after recovering from the flood, humans soon set up new political structures to serve ungodly purposes. Instead of going out to multiply and subdue the earth (the dominion mandate of Gen 1:28), they built a city to bring God to them (Gen 11:4). As a result, God dispersed humans into different areas of the world, confounding them with language differences. As humans spread out after the Tower of Babel, they developed a diverse array of political arrangements. Still, all such societies depended on some power relationship between the rulers and the ruled. In Rom 13, the apostle Paul explicitly says that God appoints governing authorities to restrain evil in human societies and promote the general good of its citizens. The Bible generally seems to assume that governments are better for protecting societies than the opposite, political anarchy. Political theorists define anarchy as the absence of higher political authority. Throughout history, where political control fails, anarchical societies have arisen and become the breeding grounds for warlords, gangs, and terrorists.

But let's be clear. While government is generally for the good of society, it remains a concession to human sinfulness. Sin is, in fact, a form of worldliness. As Glenn Tinder writes, "Original sin is the quiet determination, deep in everyone, to stay inside the world."[7] From within it, the world tends to look like it is all there is to reality, and politics may be seen as

---

6. Thucydides, *Peloponnesian War*, 351.
7. Tinder, *Political Meaning*, 41.

a way to control that reality. When dealing with politics, we deal with a genuine form of worldliness. Because of this, and because of original sin, Christians may be tempted to believe that the only way to live politically is to use worldly means to engage in it or else to retreat from politics altogether. Both options have storied histories in Christian history, including the extremes of the Crusades and monasticism. On the other hand, Daniel evokes a subtler, more nuanced approach to politics. He was engaged but separate from the society he served. His approach may help us engage in politics more wisely in our day.

Like Daniel, many people throughout history and worldwide have lived without the right to vote or publicly participate in the state's political affairs. Such societies, though certainly not all, may be hostile to Christianity or expressions of Christianity that are not approved by a state-sanctioned view of religion. In more extreme cases, the state may persecute Christian beliefs and Christians themselves. In a way, this starkly simplifies the problems and choices Christians have, though not always. Many Christians today must negotiate life in hostile political conditions and are faced with the dilemma of whether, where, when, and how to consider obeying, confronting, or disobeying political authority. Daniel faced similar challenges and exemplifies what it was like to live without the right to voluntarily participate in politics yet do so with wisdom and respect for governing authorities.

In more democratic societies, with rights of speech and political engagement, there are different challenges. First, the prevailing culture of naturalism in democratic societies frequently demands that Christians keep their faith out of public discourse. It can feel oppressive to live in a society where Christians are the odd people out, like being on a playground with school bullies running the show. It tempts us to bond closer to our Christian brothers and sisters, to those who hold our worldview, and to view and treat others as the enemy. Under these conditions, Christians sometimes seem to believe that a political right means a God-given license to say whatever they want in opposition to the dominant culture when it comes to their preferred policies, politicians, and politics. In that license, they may behave in ways that mirror un-Christian approaches to other human beings. Because Daniel attained high rank in both the Babylonian and Persian eras, he exemplifies how to think about engaging in politics while exercising our political freedom with wisdom and respect.

Daniel offers modern Christians an excellent model to consider when engaging our political world. Our times are undoubtedly tumultuous.

Whether we live in conditions of political freedom or various degrees of authoritarianism, Daniel offers us clues about how to live wisely with an understanding of a transcendent reality, the "invisible" reality of God's kingdom on earth, in real-time, in our time, wherever we live. Daniel clearly understood how to live with God's kingdom foremost in his mind while subordinating his physical and political life to it. The thesis for this work is that Daniel led an exemplary life of faith during the historical political events of his day because he was committed to God's kingdom purposes for his day. Thus, Daniel models how we may live exemplary lives of faith by committing ourselves to God's kingdom purposes for our day, even in our troubled political times.

2

Methodology: Abductive Reasoning

BEFORE EXPLORING THE BOOK of Daniel and its meaning for how we live well politically, I want to address its credibility and reliability. Is the book a genuine work of sacred Scripture? Is the author of the book an ancient Jew by the name of Daniel? While questioning the book's authenticity may seem sacrilegious to some believers, many critics openly deny its credibility or reliability. Since the Enlightenment, skeptics have derided or dismissed the book of Daniel as inauthentic because they claim it is the work of a pseudonymous Jew who wrote during the second century BC and, therefore, a work of historical fiction. Some go so far as to say that parts of the book may have been written during the sixth century and others were written during the second century, though they frequently disagree which parts were written during which century. Most critics mainly believe that the book of Daniel, or significant parts of his book, were written anonymously to encourage Jews during the traumatic reign of Antiochus IV Epiphanes, who sought to "hellenize" and persecute the Jews during his rule (175–63 BC). Some in the current evangelical community seem to be adopting a version of this interpretation.[1] The challenges to the authenticity and reliability of the book of Daniel vary, but they should be addressed.

---

1. See, for example, a critique of the books of Isaiah and Daniel in Walton and Sandy, *Lost World of Scripture*, 224–32. The problem with the authors' assessment is that they fudge on the central issue of authorship of the books; while they affirm a real Isaiah in the eighth century and the existence of Daniel in the sixth century, and they affirm God could have given them specific information in advance, the authors allow it could have been "prophetic schools" they established later as well, without providing any evidence they did. See *Lost World of Scripture*, 230–31.

There are several reasons why the book of Daniel confounds modern thinking. First, the author initially wrote the book in two different languages: Hebrew (chs. 1–2:4a and chs. 8–12) and Aramaic (chs. 2:4b–7). Second, the author employed two distinct literary genres: court narratives (chs. 1–6), and apocalyptic revelations (chs. 7–12). The use of the separate genres does not correspond with the use of the two different languages. The book also includes visions, given to the author and a king, prayers, and occasionally, a narrative of deliverance for some people. But last, apocalyptic literature—which includes both prophecies (foretelling what will happen) and apocalypse (from Greek, meaning "revelation" or "unveiling")—is likely even more troubling to modern people because, if true, it betrays the existence of something supernatural.

Traditionally, God commissioned prophets to be his spokesmen to warn his people and nearby peoples of impending discipline when they strayed from his direction. Prophecies were God's chosen means to allow his people to repent of their errors and return to him. Although Daniel never received a commission as a prophet in the traditional way, Jesus refers to him as a prophet (Matt 24:15). Daniel also acts prophetically once when he interprets Nebuchadnezzar's dream (Dan 4:29–27). However, most of Daniel's visions and dreams were apocalyptic. The book of Daniel has more apocalyptic chapters than any other book in the Old Testament. Modern skeptics doubt that God, if he exists, can reveal the future through human writers.

INTELLIGENCE ANALYSIS AND ITS ROLE IN VALIDATING THE BOOK OF DANIEL

Our information about our world is incomplete, fragmentary, ambiguous, and sometimes contradictory. We have far less information about the ancient world, which is frequently more ambiguous. The more time we are removed from a subject historically, the scarcer the information and data. The historian or archaeologist has to fill in the information gaps with many assumptions and inferences to create a coherent narrative of the past. Those narratives tend to change over time as we get more data to fill in for some of the missing information. Sometimes, those narratives change because scholars generate new assumptions, techniques, and discoveries about the past. Typically, scholars will fill in the missing data with assumptions that currently enjoy a consensus. Once established, scholars' narratives rarely change unless a worldview or paradigm shift in philosophical assumptions occurs. Only since the Enlightenment has scholarship made a significant paradigm shift.

Modern scholars hold to a paradigm of naturalism with a fairly rigid consensus. This consensus has grown steadily since the Enlightenment. Those who explicitly hold to naturalism believe that the universe contains everything needed for life to flourish. In a kind of physical determinism, some will go so far as to say that they can explain the entirety of physical phenomena from natural processes, including how we came to think and behave the way we do. Even our very thoughts may result from our chemical processes or genetic inheritance.

Most importantly, the modern consensus eliminates God from the equation of both history and processes. Therefore, when it comes to a book such as Daniel, the naturalist will likely assume that prophecy is impossible, that God does not exist, or that, if God does exist, he remains unknowable. Theists, on the other hand, may or may not accept the reliability of prophecy. Yet, if they do, they may still dismiss its validity by arguing that humans frequently lie and work to serve their own interests. Others may believe that some myths, though false, can still benefit people of faith. These varying approaches and perspectives lead to different arguments about the book of Daniel.

There is value in approaching the two primary propositions about the reliability of the book of Daniel as an intelligence problem. An intelligence problem requires an analyst to marshal the evidence, arguments, and assumptions to evaluate and support an assessment of which explanation or narrative makes the most sense of the problem. Every day, thousands of government analysts worldwide try to make sense out of indicators of what other nations and people are doing or intending to do. Analysts must process vast reams of data and information that flood them daily. Over thirty years ago, it was commonplace to say that the amount of information that US intelligence agencies received could fill the entire Library of Congress every twenty-four hours. With the advent of the internet and now the emerging "Internet of Things" (IoT), the scale of information to be addressed has increased by multiple orders of magnitude. Because of this, intelligence analysts now rely on data science, or meta-analysis, to keep abreast of the "big picture" while still attending to the smaller points of data individually.

However, trying to make sense of all the data and information involves a more complex process than we may think. The information and data in intelligence agencies are often incomplete, ambiguous, contradictory, or at least at odds with other bits of information. Requesting more information may increase the burden on the analyst trying to sift through and make sense of it without providing greater clarity. In addition to the complex problem of data and information management, analysts, like all of us, also hold beliefs or assumptions they may be unaware of and make inferences from them unconsciously.

Let me illustrate what I mean. Do facts speak for themselves? For example, imagine a man lying in the gutter. Stop and ask yourself, what's the first thing that comes to mind? When two people are presented with the same fact, something interesting occurs: they may infer different things about the same "fact," likely based on an assumption of which they may not be consciously aware.[2]

Table 1: Man Lying in a Gutter	
Good Citizen A	*Good Samaritan B*
Infers the man is a bum	Infers the man needs help
Assumes only bums lie in gutters	Assumes anyone lying in a gutter needs help

The fact of a man lying in a gutter fails to explain why he is there. When I've done this test in front of different audiences, I will hear roughly five to six different inferences, including the man is homeless, or he's taking a nap, or he's drunk. These inferences may depend upon what ideas were salient to the hearer then. For example, when taking my friend Ken on a hike recently, I presented this test to him. He immediately thought the man must have been murdered. But, after discussing it, he admitted that he had recently read a murder mystery. The idea of murder was more salient to him than other options at that moment, so it seemed to be the most reasonable cause for the man lying in the gutter. Though simple, this test illustrates how assumptions help us make sense of incomplete or fragmentary information yet may lead to varied results. We assume things based on beliefs or ideas we hold, consciously or unconsciously, about other people and the world around us.

Assumptions or beliefs form part of our cognitive landscape and mental processes. Scholars have compared human thinking to computer

---

2. See Foundation for Critical Thinking, "Inferences and Assumptions."

information processing to understand this better. In his classic study on political decision making, Robert Jervis uses cognitive psychology research to examine national leaders' rational and irrational decisions in international politics. He points out that for policymakers, just like for us, the fundamental problem remains that facts do not speak for themselves. Every human interprets facts based on some prior idea, image, belief, or theory of how things work.[3] Cognitive psychological models give researchers several hypotheses to help us understand the powers and limitations of human cognition.

Jervis highlights many things in his research, but several ideas stand out. First, people tend to be theory driven more than data driven in their thinking. Rather than attend to every fact every time, we create efficient ways of thinking about things that focus on some facts and disregard others. As we go through our education and socialization process, we develop theories or beliefs about what constitutes acceptable behavior and how and why different people and nations act the way they do. We selectively attend to or ignore information to construct our experience, as humans can only make 7 (+/− 2) discriminations on any stimulus continuum, whether colors or sounds, and can retain only that magic number of 7 (+/− 2) items in our short-term conscious memory.

We also assimilate new information into our existing beliefs. People will attend to alternative explanations until they have decided on an issue. However, once formed, our beliefs become highly resistant to change. People can usually interpret evidence to support their opinions—an experience everyone has had with someone who refuses to change his mind, regardless of the evidence. Because of this, we tend to see what we expect to see, which is both a cognitive benefit and a limitation. We benefit from this efficient way of thinking. For example, I hold to a theory that my wife loves me. And so, when I come home late at night after teaching a seminar at the university and she appears grumpy, I don't infer that I did something wrong. I infer she must have had a bad day. It's rational to continue assuming she loves me—unless she gripes at me for three consecutive months and I don't pay attention!

Mindsets, beliefs, and theories about how things work and how people behave tend to be quick to form but resistant to change. This tendency is seen in our natural habit of creating the first reasonable hypothesis about a novel situation. Scholars call this tendency "satisficing" (a neologism for

3. Jervis, *Perception*, 117–202.

sufficient and satisfying). Unless we consider alternative explanations and hypotheses thoughtfully, we may have "premature cognitive closure," leading us to develop a "hypothesis confirming bias," which leads us to look only for evidence confirming our initial hypothesis and ignore evidence contradicting it.

Such cognitive strengths and limitations need to be accounted for in the analysis. Intelligence agencies have developed various analytical tools to address these cognitive limitations.[4] These tools or techniques are a subset of social science methodology, and as such, they bring greater intellectual rigor to intelligence analysis. These techniques employ more specific and clearly defined forms of abductive reasoning. Before introducing these methods, intelligence agencies primarily relied on expert opinion—the years of experience and judgment of analysts who studied a particular subject for a long time. Expert opinion has value, but it also has limitations. Over the last thirty or more years, intelligence agencies have continually worked to improve their craft, providing analysts with more and better analytical tools to evaluate the problems they seek to address. I will use one such technique, called an Analysis of Competing Hypotheses (ACH), later in the book to help us evaluate the reliability and credibility of the book of Daniel. An ACH is useful to assess the strength of the arguments, evidence, and inferences given for the different views on a subject. I will not be evaluating the truth of the book of Daniel, per se. Still, I will evaluate the assumptions and available pieces of evidence adduced for the different hypotheses about the book of Daniel. I will also use another technique of intelligence analysis, called a Key Assumptions Check, to evaluate how the different assumptions may bias the arguments for or against the reliability of Daniel's authorship.[5]

An ACH helps us compare a set of mutually exclusive explanations or hypotheses. It involves identifying the various hypotheses, the items of evidence that support or contradict each one, and the implicit or explicit assumptions people may have and then selecting the hypothesis that best fits the evidence. I use this method to try to refute each hypothesis rather than confirm it to avoid the "hypothesis confirming bias" discussed previously. The most likely hypothesis is the one determined to have the least evidence

---

4. The first effort at this was Heuer's *Psychology of Intelligence Analysis*.

5. Heuer and Pherson, *Structured Techniques*. For the Analysis of Competing Hypotheses, see *Structured Techniques*, 181–92; for the Key Assumptions Check, see *Structured Techniques*, 209–14.

against it, not necessarily the one with the most in favor of it, though both could be true. ACH helps analysts avoid the habit of "hypothesis confirming bias" and protect against overconfidence in the first hypothesis that may lead them to see what they expect to see. It will help us as well.

Two hypotheses, particularly concerning its authorship, are under contention for the book of Daniel. They are depicted below as hypothesis 1 (H_1) and hypothesis 2 (H_2):

H_1: The book of Daniel was written by a single author in the sixth century BC.

H_2: The book of Daniel was written by an anonymous Jew in the second century BC.

As we will see, some implicit and explicit assumptions are critical to these hypotheses. The ACH process will make those implicit assumptions explicit and test whether these drive the assessment of the hypotheses or the evidence drives the assessment.

An illustrative sample of the ACH matrix appears in table 2 below. There are lines for evidence and arguments for and against each hypothesis. I include both confirming and disconfirming evidence for each one. In addition, intelligence analysts must assess the credibility of the evidence, and we will do so here as well. Not all evidence is of equal value because the analyst must also consider the believability or reliability of the source of the evidence—whether it is testimonial, documentary, technical, or interpretive.[6]

Assumptions will be evaluated as well. Assumptions, however, do not rely on credibility the way evidence does, but each assumption must be reasonable and justified by the person holding to the belief. Additionally, assumptions should be made explicit. Unfortunately, many authors fail to do this.

As an illustration of what will come in the last chapter, I use a matrix to analyze the two hypotheses. In the sample matrix below, there are lines of evidence. I evaluate the credibility of the evidence based on a probability system used by intelligence agencies known as the Fuzzy System; it is listed in table 11 in the last chapter. Under each hypothesis a "1" will appear if that line of evidence supports that hypothesis and a "-1" if it contradicts that hypothesis. The actual spreadsheet for the ACH appears separately as

---

6. For a good summary of how evidence, credibility, and believability can be understood in the intelligence process, see chs. 1–7 of Tecuci et al., *Intelligence Analysis*.

appendix A. If any individual piece of evidence can fit both hypotheses, it will be rejected as nondiagnostic for our assessment. That is to say, if one piece of evidence supports or contradicts all hypotheses simultaneously, it cannot help determine the best hypothesis or rule out the weakest one. Something that explains everything ultimately explains nothing.

Table 2: Sample Analyses of Competing Hypotheses				
Item	Evidence	Credibility	H_1	H_2
1	Written in two languages	Almost certain	1	1
2	Imperial Aramaic style	Very likely	1	-1
3	Hebrew purpose	Very likely	1	-1
4	Fifth-century Aramaic	Almost certain	1	-1

Keep in mind that assumptions work differently than evidence. Evaluating evidence is based on whether it's true, whereas assumptions are based on whether they are useful. The truth of an assumption is not at issue. For example, in a particular international relations theory known as neorealism, theorists assume that nations are "rational actors." Of course, nations are not single, unitary actors. There are many actors and agencies in the government's service, and they often work at cross purposes. However, the assumption of rationality helps simplify the theory and support its usefulness, even though we know that not all political leaders and agencies are always rational. For these reasons and others, we will separately evaluate the critical assumptions of each hypothesis.

Does this type of approach work? You have probably heard of "intelligence failures." Probably the two greatest intelligence failures in our generation have been the failure to anticipate the terrorist attacks of 9/11 and the estimate of Iraqi weapons of mass destruction that explicitly said Saddam Hussein was continuing his pursuit of nuclear, biological, and chemical weapons (see appendix C, "Intelligence Failure"). So why use an intelligence assessment of the book of Daniel? I use this approach primarily because the methods employed by the intelligence community typically are more self-correcting than mere argumentation and can provide an inventory of arguments and evidence for a "postmortem" analysis if the assessment subsequently proves incorrect. Analysts especially value this type of audit trail when events overcome their anticipation of or failure to anticipate certain events or processes. However, the internal process of critically thinking about how they understand or assess the problem has inherent value in helping them reveal their thought processes about something.

An Analysis of Competing Hypotheses is a specific form of abductive reasoning. Abductive reasoning is one type within the scientific method that includes deduction and induction. Deductive reasoning seeks to show that something is necessarily true and follows from the assumptions and axioms in the premises. Inductive reasoning, conversely, seeks to show that something is probably true by testing hypotheses against the available evidence, much of which may be generated by experimentation. Based on the available evidence, abductive reasoning, reasoning to the best explanation, tries to show what is possibly or most likely true. Most physical sciences rely on the deductive form of theoretical reasoning, while the acceptability of the theory is empirically tested (primarily through inductive methods).[7] Most of the work in intelligence, on the other hand, works with abductive reasoning, reasoning to the best hypothesis.

Most people who argue for or against the authorship of the book of Daniel follow the deductive form. However, they only partially follow the scientific method in testing against the available evidence, as we only have minimal evidence on questions of historical reliability and cannot generate experiments to develop new evidence. Evangelicals, theists, nontheists, and skeptics hold to different theories or assumptions about what is possible, and these tend to drive their search for evidence and explanations of evidence that confirm or disconfirm their hypothesis. Abductively assessing the available evidence, assumptions, and arguments helps us determine the best explanation.

The full "assessment" of the reliability of Daniel's book may be found in the last chapter. It will be a lengthier assessment than what is typically given to policymakers, who generally have little time to read full assessments from the intelligence community and, therefore, rarely want them. Since they often pose the questions, they want a crisp, bottom-line, up-front (BLUF) answer backed by two or three of the most robust lines of evidence supporting it. Policymakers also want to know what level of confidence analysts have in their intelligence assessment. My evaluation may be helpful for those who would enjoy an apologetic answer to skeptics of the book of Daniel. For those who don't, feel free to skip it or save it for a later date.

---

7. For a discussion of research methodology, see Telhami, *Power and Leadership*, 20–21.

My BLUF? I assess that the authorship of the book of Daniel by a real person in the sixth century BC is more reliably accurate than the competing hypothesis. It has greater explanatory power than the alternative hypothesis that the book was written by an anonymous Jew living in the second century BC. I evaluate Daniel's career in Babylon based on this assessment.

THE STRUCTURE OF THE BOOK

The chapters that follow will allow us to dig into the political and spiritual life of Daniel using abductive reasoning where the textual or historical evidence is not clear. In chapter 3, we will begin with a brief history and context of his life, where I propose to show how Daniel somehow survived the trauma of being forced to be uprooted from his native land and serve in the court of Babylon. In addition, we will examine the likely means by which he was spared from trauma by committing to serve God's kingdom purposes in exile. I will assess how God may have provided a "way of escape" from the trauma through the experience of the capture and forced service. Reasons why he might have been delivered and the means of how he was delivered are the key themes of this chapter. We will also evaluate how Daniel understood God's sovereign rule over politics.

In chapters 4 through 8, we will discuss a variety of appeals Daniel made while serving in Babylon. These appeals reveal a person with very high regard for God's sovereign rule over his kingdom and the whole universe and a high view of the political authority of human kingdoms and the authority of the kingdom of God. The quality of his appeals will be evaluated through the prism of five questions that will address each of his appeals. We will use abductive reasoning to tease out the nuances of his appeals. The five questions are,

1. How does Daniel prepare ahead of time?
2. What are the positive elements of Daniel's appeal?
3. What makes his appeal attractive or appealing?
4. How does he expertly phrase his appeal?
5. How does he maintain submission to authority through his appeal?

Chapter 4 will examine Daniel's first appeal for a restricted diet of vegetables while beginning what we might think of as a three-year master's degree program in Babylonian administration, including the language

METHODOLOGY: ABDUCTIVE REASONING

and literature of the Chaldeans. The focus of chapter 5 will be to examine Daniel's appeal to the commander of Nebuchadnezzar's bodyguards to have time to interpret the king's dream, sparing himself and others from the sure sentence of death the king ordered on all the wise men at the time. Chapter 6 will evaluate why Daniel appealed to King Darius without words, which led Daniel to the lion's den. Chapter 7 will evaluate Daniel's prayer of appeal to God to restore Judah to its ancestral homeland. Chapter 8 will evaluate Daniel's appeal to an angel for more detailed information about the last revelation given to him. As mentioned, chapter 9 will contain my ACH assessment of the book of Daniel's reliability and the critical assumptions used by the two approaches. As we work through these chapters, I hope you, as the reader, will learn how Daniel wisely followed God's kingdom purposes for his day while in a politically hostile land. But first, we turn to how Daniel may have navigated the trauma of captivity and understood God's sovereign control over history.

3

God's Sovereign Rule with Daniel in Babylon

Earlier, we noted that sin is a form of worldliness. "Worldliness" means the sense that the world and all it contains is the only reality to consider. The worldliness of politics seems to have few bounds, with constant striving for power. The worldliness of Abel killing Cain plays out within and between political societies, in civil wars, and wars between states and nations as men seek to gain power to control others for their interests. Christians have had to reckon with the paradoxical nature of human beings: destined for glory by the God of heaven yet bedeviled with sin. In a concession to human sinfulness, there may be no other option than to provide for governance. But how do we understand God's sovereign role in history through this political governance? Believers and unbelievers alike are constrained by the politics of their day wherever they have lived, and political forces at work can seem overwhelming. This may be the hardest to understand in international politics.

Political entities of different sizes and configurations have existed throughout history. Such entities take many different forms, but they share some commonalities. They all seek to advance society, maintain a unique identity, and obtain resources. Whether tribes, clans, city-states, empires, feudal monarchies, or even nation-states, all have vied for control to conquer others and prevent themselves from being conquered. Small, medium, and great powers fight for control when victory looks likely, ally with one another to defend against conquest where possible, or live in the shadow of larger powers, frequently being compelled to submit to the larger power's political agenda. This struggle for control was no different during Daniel's time.

Daniel was born in the small state of Judah, probably around 620 BC.[1] Daniel lived during the reign of three great powers, from about 620 to sometime after 539 BC. He witnessed the end of Assyria (612 BC), the rise and fall of Babylon (612–539 BC), and the early reign of Persia (539 BC). Egypt lost its luster but remained a larger regional power than Judah and the smaller nations around it. As a medium-sized power, Egypt worked to keep from being conquered by Assyria and later Babylon. At the same time, it also provided unreliable and often fickle protection for the much smaller state of Judah.[2]

More than one hundred years before Babylon came to take Daniel and his friends, the Assyrian Empire destroyed the northern Kingdom of Israel (722 BC). After the conquest, the Assyrians systematically forced the best and brightest citizens of the conquered lands to be relocated to different parts of their empire while also colonizing the new territory by relocating some Assyrians to the conquered lands. In doing so, Assyria essentially wiped the Israelite nation off the map as a functioning political entity. Only the tribes of Judah and Benjamin were left, a remnant of God's covenant. This Assyrian policy helped prevent rebellions from conquered peoples. For subsequent history in Palestine, however, this practice led to a schism between the remaining Israelites in the north and the Jews of the southern Kingdom. The Israelites, who remained in what was later called Samaria, intermarried with the Assyrians and adopted many of their pagan gods and religious practices. Jews from Judah looked down on the "Samaritans" as compromisers, utterly undeserving of their respect.[3]

Once the Babylonians came to power, they repeated the Assyrian practice of forced migrations, though with a twist. The Babylonians imported people to serve in their courts or as laborers for many construction projects. Instead of relocating large populations, however, the Babylonians took only those they needed for specific projects to avoid overcrowding and other problems associated with mass migrations (such as sanitation, water and food supplies, and housing).[4] This also helped preclude the development of ghettos, with all their attendant health problems. Babylon allowed

---

1. Archer, *Encyclopedia*, 284.
2. Seymour, *Babylon*, 47; see also Bruce, *Israel and the Nations*, 78–79.
3. Bruce, *Israel and the Nations*, 78–79.
4. Ahn, *Exile*, 32–33.

ethnic enclaves to develop over time per available jobs, housing, and capacity. Enclaves of dispersed Jews who arrived over several migrations helped newer immigrants assimilate into Babylonian society.[5]

Once it set its eyes on Judah, Babylon forcibly removed Jews three if not four times over more than twenty-five years. The first forced migration occurred in 605 BC when Nebuchadnezzar defeated Pharaoh Neco of Egypt at Carchemish. It involved only a few people, one of whom was Daniel. Egypt's loss to Babylon meant that Judah lost its independence. Babylon made Judah part of its western province, while Daniel and his three friends were taken to serve in the court of Babylon. It is possible that more were taken in this first migration, but the Scriptures remain silent. Nebuchadnezzar's army also took some of the temple treasury.[6] These thefts fulfilled Isaiah's prophecy to King Hezekiah for having foolishly let the Babylonian envoys see the wealth of Judah nearly a century before (Isa 39:7). The book of Daniel doesn't address the subsequent forced migrations that occurred in 597, 586, and 582 BC, but they are recorded in 2 Kgs 24, Jer 39–43, and Pss 79 and 137. The most destructive of these migrations was the third one in 586 BC, as Babylon destroyed the city of Jerusalem and the temple for Judah's rebellion. No longer would Jews worship at the temple. They began a new practice of worshipping in synagogues, a tradition still today.

What about Daniel and his friends' migration? The few texts we have on their journey indicate something powerful may have happened, something we should avoid glossing over. One scholar suggests that the study of the Babylonian exile remains incomplete if it fails to address the personal and intergenerational trauma that may have occurred during these forced migration and exile in a foreign land.[7] Trauma is the key. For those who suffer trauma from whatever source, it is overwhelming, unbearable, and almost impossible to comprehend. It may be difficult to fully grasp what these young men, perhaps still boys, experienced, yet we do them and the text an injustice if we fail to try. It takes a bit of thoughtfulness on our part to get into the sandals of Daniel and his friends as they were forcibly taken from their families and homes in Judah. They were likely no more than fifteen years old.[8]

The Babylonian caravan, traveling with captured booty and people to the city of Babylon, may have taken as long as four months via the regular

---

5. Kriwaczek, *Babylon*, 170–71, 260–61.
6. Bruce, *Israel and the Nations*, 80.
7. See Southwood, review of *Exile*, 277–81.
8. Archer, *Encyclopedia*, 284.

trade route. The route they would have traveled moved in an arc northward up the coast of the Levant, eastward toward Asshur, and southward toward Babylon along the road just west of the Euphrates River, a distance of about nine hundred miles.[9] Their travel becomes important later when we evaluate how they may have been able to deal with their trauma. After being forcibly taken from their homes in Judah, the boys were stripped of their personal and ethnic identity by being given pagan names after the gods of Babylon. This renaming of people to change their identities in their new homeland has gone on for millennia in the hope of changing the conquered peoples' loyalties. Throughout history, empires have used this and other techniques to force assimilation into the new culture and political life.

The Jews who experienced forced migration most certainly experienced trauma. The forced exile to Babylon radically changed their identity as Jews. Psalm 137 gives insight into this trauma through a lament of what life was like in Babylon, at least for the Jews deported in the second forced migration in 597 BC:

> By the rivers of Babylon we sat and wept
> > when we remembered Zion.
> There on the poplars
> > we hung our harps,
> for there our captors asked us for songs,
> > our tormentors demanded songs of joy;
> > they said "Sing us one of the songs of Zion!"
>
> How can we sing the songs of the LORD
> > while in a foreign land?
> If I forget you, Jerusalem,
> > may my right hand forget its skill.
> May my tongue cling to the roof of my mouth
> > if I do not remember you,
> if I do not consider Jerusalem
> > my highest joy.
>
> Remember, LORD, what the Edomites did
> > on the day Jerusalem fell.
> "Tear it down," they cried,
> > "tear it down to its foundations."
> Daughter Babylon, doomed to destruction,
> > happy is he who repays you

---

9. *ESV Study Bible*, 799; cf. Bruce, *Israel and the Nations*, 79.

> according to what you have done to us.
> Happy is the one who seizes your infants
> and dashes them against the rocks.

This record and the gruesome, vengeful wish of the psalmist suggest the trauma of the captivity: the psalmist portrays himself and other Jews as tormented victims and longs for vengeance on Babylon and others.

Marginal notes in one of my NIV study Bibles indicate that this psalmist was back in Jerusalem when he composed this psalm.[10] The psalmist, though now back in Jerusalem, remains stuck in the past, reliving the experience more than remembering it. Further, notice that the psalmist never refers to any of the prophecies given by Isaiah, Jeremiah, and others about God's displeasure with the Jews for abandoning him. The psalmist's recollection has all the hallmarks of what we now call PTSD, which stands for post-traumatic stress disorder. These hallmarks may include intrusive images, flashbacks, nightmares, depression, and uncontrollable anxiety. Observers have noted for some time the effect that wars can have on soldiers who have experienced wartime brutality, having called it over the years "war neurosis," "shell shock," and "battle fatigue." These observations go back throughout history through all wars and across all cultures. But it's not only war that causes trauma, interpersonal violence, child abuse, severe childhood neglect, sexual assault, slavery, and more may induce trauma. Forced migration, which resembles kidnapping, causes it as well.

Trauma research has increased and advanced significantly since the Vietnam War. Many psychologists, psychiatrists, and neurologists have been doing extraordinary work in understanding how trauma affects the minds, brains, and bodies of those who suffer from it. One of the leading contemporary researchers into trauma and PTSD, Bessel van der Kolk, makes an important observation about this kind of trauma: "I am continually impressed by how difficult it is for people who have gone through the unspeakable to convey the essence of their experience. It is so much easier for them to talk about what has been done to them—to tell a story of victimization and revenge—than to notice, feel, and put into words the reality of their internal experience."[11]

Those who suffer from PTSD are trapped in the past and cannot find a way forward. It is "the result of a fundamental reorganization of the central nervous system based on having experienced an actual threat

---

10. Barker et al., *NIV Study Bible*, 930.
11. van der Kolk, *Body*, 47.

of annihilation (or seeing someone else being annihilated), which reorganizes self-experience (as helpless) and the interpretation of reality (the entire world is a dangerous place)."[12] Being trapped in the past also has other effects. First, it causes the sufferers to strongly identify with those who share the trauma (in the book of Daniel, other relocated Jews) as opposed to those who don't share that bond, including those Jews who were left behind in Palestine as well as sympathetic Babylonians. Second, those stuck in the past due to PTSD lose the ability to imagine a better future or a way forward from the trauma. "Not being fully alive in the present keeps them more firmly imprisoned in the past."[13] For them, the past remains an ever-present reality.

Why did this happen? God was disciplining the Judeans for having forsaken him. Jeremiah 5:18–19 harshly rebukes God's people for their folly. The text says, "Yet even in those days . . . I will not destroy you completely. And when the people ask, 'Why has the LORD our God done all this to us?' you will tell them, 'As you have forsaken me and served foreign gods in your own land, so now you will serve foreigners in a land not your own.'" Jeremiah 7:9–10 accuses them of stealing, murdering, adultery, perjury, burning incense to Baal, following other gods, and hypocritically coming before God himself, believing they were immune to being disciplined by him. Jer 7:30–31 further charges them with setting up idols in God's temple and sacrificing their sons and daughters to pagan gods. Their practices were called abominable.

The prophets gave the Jews plenty of warning about the consequences of disobeying God. Instead of responding to God in faith, many of these Jews seemed to wallow in their misery. And, like their counterparts back home in Judah, they would believe false prophets who promised them deliverance if they would rebel against Babylon. Instead, in Jer 29:4–9, God gave them hope that if they settled down in Babylon—built houses, planted gardens, married, and had children—they would prosper along with Babylon. And they were to seek the peace and prosperity of Babylon, even while it ruled over them, and ignore prophets who falsely told them to rebel against Babylonian rule.

Few commentators assess what may have happened to Daniel and his friends physically that could have significantly compounded their trauma. The Scriptures give us a clue. The prophecy Isaiah gave to Hezekiah in Isa

---

12. van der Kolk, *Body*, 256.
13. van der Kolk, *Body*, 67.

39:5–7, after he foolishly allowed Babylonian visitors to view the wealth of Judah,[14] specified what would happen:

> Then Isaiah said to Hezekiah, "Hear the word of the LORD Almighty: The time will surely come when everything in your palace, and all that your predecessors have stored up until this day, will be carried off to Babylon. Nothing will be left, says the LORD. And some of your descendants, your own flesh and blood who will be born to you, will be taken away, and they will become *eunuchs* in the palace of the king of Babylon." (emphasis added)

The book of Daniel records the prophecy coming true. In Dan 1:1–3a, we see a partial fulfillment of this prophecy:

> In the third year of the reign of Jehoiakim king of Judah, Nebuchadnezzar king of Babylon came to Jerusalem and besieged it. And the LORD delivered Jehoiakim king of Judah into his hand, along with some of the articles from the temple of God. These he carried off to the temple of his god in Babylonia and put in the treasure house of his god. Then the king ordered Ashpenaz, chief of his *court officials*, to bring in some of the Israelites from the royal family and nobility. (emphasis added)

Daniel, and perhaps his friends, were royal descendants of Hezekiah's lineage. Further, the Hebrew word translated as "court officials" is *sarasim*, the plural word for eunuchs, the same word used in Isaiah's prophecy. Many translations tend to substitute euphemisms for this term. The custom and practice of making men into eunuchs to serve in the court of kings was common among the ancient Assyrian, Babylonian, Persian, and Chinese Empires. More frequently than not, the boy's or man's genitals were bound up, and the testes were *dragged* or *crushed* without anesthesia. Sometimes they would cut off the testicles or the penis, and sometimes both. Sadly, eunuchs were held in contempt by the very people who forcibly mutilated them, especially if they were conquered foreigners. Nonetheless, many of these eunuchs would rise in service to the king.

The agony and cruelty of emasculation is hard to imagine. Indeed, it may be why few commentators address the topic, or when they do, they gloss over it. It may also be why so many translations substitute terms like "court officials," as here. Scholars have paid little attention to the role (or trauma) of eunuchs in the ancient world, but we have an intriguing glimpse

---

14. One scholar believes the Babylonian rulers were attempting to divert Assyrian attention away from Babylon and to Palestine. See Oates, *Babylon*, 116.

into this practice from ancient China. Scholar Bruce Gerig quotes from an ancient source: "Sunia Qian (Ssu-ma Chein, 145-ca. 90 BC), who was 'sent to the silkhouse' to be castrated after being accused of attempting to mislead the Chinese emperor, wrote eight years later how he still sat 'in a daze,' sweat drenching his clothes as he thought of his shame and wishing only that he could 'hide away in the furthest depths of the mountains.' Still, Qian went on to become the Grand Historian of the Han Court."[15] Sunia Qian suffered from what we today call PTSD, reliving the effects of the past in the present. Despite his great success, he lived with humiliating shame and no escape from the trauma that continued to shake him physically, mentally, and emotionally.

There is a comparable type of trauma today worldwide, which is female genital mutilation (FGM). According to the World Health Organization (WHO), about two hundred million women living today have been genitally mutilated. Another three million women are being added to that number annually.[16] These mutilations offer no medical benefit whatsoever to the victims. Still, there are multiple, lifelong, adverse physical and psychological consequences to the women who have been forced to submit to it or to observe it. Such symptoms include depression, anxiety, and other psychological problems. Multiple studies have shown these women are at higher risk of PTSD, and we would expect the same to be true of males who have suffered similar trauma.

Trauma and PTSD researchers have made significant advancements with the development of new scientific disciplines. New technologies and techniques (PET scans—positron emission tomography, and fMRIs—functional magnetic resonance imagery) have allowed researchers in these disciplines to see what occurs in the brain and nervous system of people affected by trauma. These new disciplines include "neuroscience, the study of how the brain supports mental processes; developmental psychopathology, the study of the impact of adverse experiences of the development of mind and brain; and interpersonal neurobiology, the study of how our behavior influences the emotions, biology, and mind-sets of those around us."[17] The research reveals that trauma of all kinds induces fundamental physiological changes in the brains and bodies of its victims. In his classic work *The Body Keeps the Score*, van der Kolk adds, "These changes explain why

---

15. See Gerig, "Eunuchs," para. 1.
16. See WHO, "Female Genital Mutilation," para. 7.
17. van der Kolk, *Body*, 2.

traumatized individuals become hypervigilant to threat at the expense of spontaneously engaging in their day-to-day lives. They also help us understand why traumatized people so often keep repeating the same problems and have such trouble learning from their experience."[18] However, trauma affects the brain and physiology of each person differently. Not all people who have experienced trauma suffer from PTSD.

Daniel doesn't say that he and his friends were emasculated. However, Daniel would have no reason to mention it. For a Jew, stigma and shame would be attached to the very word. In Deut 23:1, the law forbids an emasculated male from participating in the "assembly of the Lord." Not only would a eunuch be unable to participate in the community's religious life, but he would also be unable to produce heirs, something highly valued in Jewish culture. According to Lev 22:24–25, the law also forbids animals with damaged or deformed testicles to be used in animal sacrifices, demonstrating the unacceptability of those so damaged.

While Jewish law sounds harsh, it may have been a means of protecting Israel from adopting this foreign practice, which was rampant throughout the region. Nonetheless, it had the effect of stigmatizing those who were involuntarily subjected to it. The book of Daniel never indicates whether Daniel ever married or had children. It can be inferred, however, that these young men had been forcibly castrated. Most Jewish rabbinic scholars and early Christians believe this to be the case.[19]

Perhaps this indignity explains why Isaiah later prophesied in Isa 56:3–5 something extraordinary for eunuchs: "Let no foreigner who is bound to the Lord say, 'The Lord will surely exclude me from his people.' And let no eunuch complain, 'I am only a dry tree.' For this is what the Lord says: 'To the eunuchs who keep my Sabbaths, who choose what pleases me and hold fast to my covenant—to them I will give within my temple and its walls a memorial and a name better than sons and daughters; I will give them an everlasting name that will endure forever.'"

The text is especially intriguing since a eunuch could not have heirs. Still, the prophecy promises a memorial and a name better than sons and daughters, which would surely be a blessing to an involuntarily castrated Jew.

Unlike the composer of Ps 137, who longed for vengeance against his captors, Daniel and his three friends found a way to overcome these

---

18. van der Kolk, *Body*, 3.

19. Isa 37:7; see also Gerig, *Eunuchs*, para. 3; Jerome, *Commentary on Daniel*, 20; Josephus, *History of the Jews*, 937–38.

traumatic experiences. The trauma of the forced separation from their families and homeland, the long migration to a foreign land, and the stripping of their Jewish identities by being given new, pagan names, along with the likelihood of being castrated as young men, would have been sufficient to cause severe and enduring anxiety and depression, if not PTSD. However, we observe no evidence in Daniel's writings that either Daniel or his friends remained stuck in the past, demonstrated victimhood, or sought revenge. We see the opposite: lives characterized by righteousness, submission to governing authorities, reliance on God, and a sense of purpose. Why were Daniel and his friends different?

We may find some insight from van der Kolk, who notes several ways trauma can be overcome. He describes three modern approaches therapists use to help people overcome trauma and suggests that each traumatized person may need one or more of these therapies to deal with the effects of their experience: "1) top down, by talking, (re-)connecting with others, and allowing themselves to know and understand what is going on inside them, while processing the memories of the trauma; 2) by taking medicines that shut down inappropriate alarm reactions, or by utilizing other technologies that change the way the brain organizes information, and 3) bottom up: by allowing the body to have experiences that deeply and viscerally contradict the helplessness, rage, or collapse that result from trauma."[20]

The modern pharmacological approach would have been unavailable to Daniel and his friends. The first and third approaches may have been the ways these young men navigated their trauma and developed a healthy course of action.

The "top-down" approach, which involves talking and reconnecting with others, seems indicated in the text of Daniel chapters 1 and 2. Daniel, Hananiah, Mishael, and Azariah had close friendships, a shared experience of captivity, and a personal community of fellow believers with shared experiences. Daniel 2 also indicates that they prayed together, perhaps as they had learned to do after being taken from Judah on the road to Babylon. We know that Daniel read and paid attention to Scriptures, particularly the book of Jeremiah (see Dan 9:2). Van der Kolk states that traumatized human beings recover in the context of close relationships and "having a good support network [which] constitutes the single more powerful protection against being traumatized."[21] Daniel and his friends shared their experienc-

20. van der Kolk, *Body*, 3.
21. van der Kolk, *Body*, 210.

es, and it appears from Dan 2 that their support network was deepened by praying for one another. "Feeling listened to and understood changes our physiology.... Silence reinforces the godforsaken isolation of trauma."[22]

The third, "bottom-up" physical approach may have helped as well. As the caravan carried booty and captives back to Babylon over a route of about nine hundred miles, these four young friends likely had to walk a great deal. And walking has a potent therapeutic effect. One of the more effective treatments for PTSD and other forms of trauma was recently discovered by a research psychologist while taking a walk herself. One day in 1987, Francine Shapiro walked through a park, thinking about some distressing situations. She noticed that her rapid eye movements while walking greatly reduced the stress associated with those memories. She began to consider a new technique, now familiarly known as Eye Movement Desensitization and Reprocessing (EMDR). She then began to incorporate EMDR into her clinical practice. She discovered that it was a component of a much quicker and more effective treatment for helping trauma victims overcome their past.[23] The treatment includes talking (the first approach) and eye movement (the third approach). It has been so well researched since her discovery that the American Psychiatric Association, the US Department of Defense, and the Department of Veterans Affairs recommend it for treating trauma.[24] Having close friends who shared a common traumatic experience and walking toward Babylon may have helped them focus on the future and take agency of their lives during their captivity.

Taking personal responsibility, or agency, for their recovery allowed them to focus and direct their energies in a way that honored God. Taking agency requires people to acknowledge that they have both capabilities and choices. The capabilities were those internal resources Daniel and his friends had built up by studying the Scriptures; the choice had already been made to follow the Lord. These four young men show an unswerving resolve to trust in the Lord their God, demonstrate righteousness and wisdom, and humbly obey the governmental authorities of Babylon. Yet, they also kept a level of separation (boundaries) from the pagan religion and culture of Babylon. Such boundaries are difficult to maintain. If not for their already strong commitment to the Lord God as they headed into a spiritually desolate place, they likely would not have held the line.

22. van der Kolk, *Body*, 232.
23. Shapiro, *EMDR*.
24. See EMDR Institute, "History."

Of course, we don't know what happened. No text specifies their upbringing or their background, let alone how they managed to deal with everything leading up to their captivity. They appear to us in Dan 1, having already come into Babylon and already in the preparation process for the king's service. They likely shared and retained a deep knowledge of the Scriptures and their tradition while on the trip, even after being forced into Babylonian service. They may have known Isaiah's prophecies, foretelling that royal descendants of Hezekiah would be taken captive to Babylon. We certainly see, later in the book, that Daniel meticulously studied the prophecies of Jeremiah. Thus, it seems reasonable that they could have also drawn hope for themselves from the prophecies of Isaiah.

These prophecies were given about a century before the rise of Babylon. Isaiah prophesied what would happen to the descendants of Hezekiah and the people of Judah based on their disobedience. Daniel and his friends likely saw the rise of Babylon as the fulfillment of Isaiah's prophecy and Judah's suffering in a Gentile land as God's discipline. They likely saw God's sovereignty in action internationally (with the rise of Babylon), nationally (with what happened to Judah), and personally (they were descendants of Hezekiah, taken captive). Would Daniel and his friends have also remembered Isa 49:6, which gives hope for dark times that were now upon them? The text says, "It is too small a thing for you to be my servant to restore the tribes of Jacob and bring back those of Israel I have kept. I will also make you a light for the Gentiles, that my salvation may reach to the ends of the earth." This astounding passage would likely have intrigued Daniel and his friends, whose destinies were entirely out of their control. They were being forced, along with a sizeable portion of Judah in subsequent migrations, to become a "light for the Gentiles." They had a choice to submit to God and fulfill his promises personally. And, should they submit to God, they could be in a position to help "restore the tribes of Jacob." Additionally, by preserving the remnant of Judah, the line of Jesus would bring about God's salvation and take the gospel to the ends of the earth, a task we continue to complete even today.

Isaiah 49:6 has echoes in 1 Pet 3:15–16a: "But in your hearts revere Christ as Lord. Always be prepared to give an answer to everyone who asks you to give the reason for the hope that you have. But do this with gentleness and respect, keeping a clear conscience." Daniel and his friends were determined to sanctify the Lord God in their hearts in a hostile land. They must have purposefully determined, perhaps during the journey to Babylon, to follow the Lord and set themselves apart in their hearts and minds, even as they were forbidden to participate in the life of their familiar religious community, centered at the temple in Jerusalem. From the promises for eunuchs seen in Isa 56, they would have drawn hope for a future in relationship with God as they lived in the present, in obedience to him. Little did they know how greatly God would honor and prosper them in captivity.

GOD'S SOVEREIGN RULE OVER ALL THINGS

Like Daniel, we are all subject to God's sovereignty. Every day, in many areas of our lives, God's sovereign rule exerts its influence over each one of us, whether through the loss of a loved one, a change in our health, or an opportunity for a new career we didn't anticipate. (Daniel certainly couldn't have expected his career trajectory.) God's sovereign rule exerts constraints and opportunities for us, providing us with resources to accomplish his earthly purposes.

Scripture clarifies that God exercises sovereign control over his creation and describes at least five or six levels of control. The higher levels affect or place boundaries on each lower level to serve the purposes of God in ordaining all things. From the top down, God established his kingdom and all the created beings in it; he created the physical universe and all that it contains with invariant laws of physics; he created humans and orders their subsequent ways of governing themselves; God sovereignly rules over the rise and fall of individual political leaders, and of course, he sovereignly rules over each one of us. From the highest to the lowest level of sovereignty, each level provides constraints on and opportunities for what we can do as individuals.

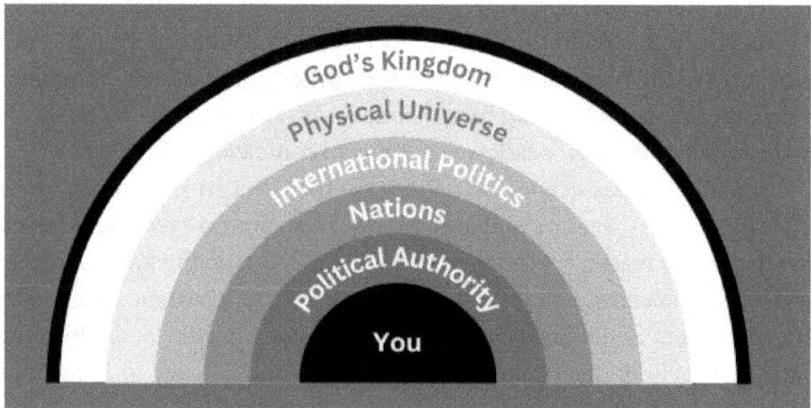

Figure 1: Levels of God's Sovereign Rule

On what basis does God's sovereignty rest? It rests on his great and holy character and creative power. Since there is no one greater than him, there is no appeal for arbitration beyond him, and he consults with no one about his decisions and their justness, for he wisely and justly rules all that he creates. He creates and rules from his character and wisdom.

God first created his kingdom for purposes he decided. His kingdom transcends the dimensions of space and time beyond our physical cosmos. As Ps 103:19 says, "The LORD has established his throne in heaven, and his kingdom rules over all." All of what? Well, for starters, it is all about what exists in the transcendent kingdom of heaven and also about the affairs of the subsequently created cosmos. His kingdom rule includes angelic beings, created before the physical creation (Job 38:7). The psalmist adds in Ps 103:20–22, "Praise the LORD, you his angels, you mighty ones who do his bidding, who obey his word. Praise the LORD, all his heavenly hosts, you his servants who do his will. Praise the LORD, all his works, everywhere in his dominion. Praise the LORD, my soul." God constrains the disobedient or fallen angels to only what he allows. We get a glimpse of this in Job 1:12, where God permits Satan to test Job: "The LORD said to Satan, 'Very well, then, everything he has is in your hands, but on the man himself do not lay a finger. Then Satan went out from the presence of the LORD." Satan went on to torment Job, but only for so long and only so far as God allowed. From his kingdom, God calls on us to reign with him over his creation and to actively pray for his will to be done on earth as his will is being done in heaven (Matt 6:10).

Second, God created the cosmos and sovereignly rules over it. Scripture makes clear in Gen 1, John 1, Job, Ps 104, and others that he created the entire cosmos and the laws of physics that do his bidding. Those physical laws define what created life can do in all its intricate variety. We are both constrained by and benefit from those various laws for eating, reproducing, working, and playing. The constraints of those physical laws are generally observable in the created realm. Children learn their rudiments through experience and from parents who teach them to avoid falling off ladders, touching fires, and the like. Animals learn from their parents and are aided by instincts. One cannot simply walk off a cliff's ledge and disobey the law of gravity. God builds in these constraints and opportunities to limit the expression of evil, to enhance human life, and, ultimately, to bring humans into intimate relationships with himself.[25] The apostle Paul tells us that

25. Ross, *Universe*, 183–206.

creation contains enough evidence to infer God's divine attributes and power and come to acknowledge him (Rom 1:19–20).

Third, God sovereignly rules over what we would call international politics, which is the diplomatic, economic, and military interplay of political entities over time. In the past, it might have been called inter-imperial or inter-tribal politics, but it's all the same idea. States, empires, and other political entities constrain one another in their actions internationally or regionally, depending on their relative military power. Political entities can only extend their domain at the expense of others, and others can effectively blunt those encroachments by building up their internal military resources or allying with other threatened entities to block them. Yet God sovereignly rules over them all, "for dominion belongs to the LORD and he rules over the nations" (Ps 22:28). Psalm 33:10–11 goes further and says that God can change the trajectory of nations to suit his purposes: "The LORD foils the plans of the nations; he thwarts the purposes of the peoples. But the plans of the LORD stand firm forever, the purposes of his heart through all generations." Beyond the evidence he left in the physical world of his attributes and power, God wills that people will come to acknowledge him through even their geographical and historical contexts. As Acts 17:26–27 says, "From one man he made all the nations, that they should inhabit the whole earth; and he marked out their appointed times in history and the boundaries of their lands. God did this so that they would seek him and perhaps reach out for him and find him, though he is not far from any one of us."

Fourth, God sovereignly rules over individual nations, though this may be hard to discern sometimes as a citizen of any one of them. Political theorists have yet to provide a reliable hypothesis of what makes nations powerful and what causes their fall from power. But God rules nations to serve his purposes. As Dan 2:21 says, "He changes times and seasons; he deposes kings and raises up others." Job 12:23 adds that God "makes nations great, and destroys them; he enlarges nations and disperses them." The king of Babylon, Nebuchadnezzar, eventually recognized this after a brief bout of insanity. Beyond reason, he proudly boasted of his political accomplishments, failing to acknowledge that God had ordained his rule and successes. In Dan 4:34–35, the king says, "At the end of that time, I, Nebuchadnezzar, raised my eyes toward heaven, and my sanity was restored. Then I praised the Most High; I honored and glorified him who lives forever. His dominion is an eternal dominion; his kingdom endures from generation to generation. All the peoples of the earth are regarded as nothing. He does as he pleases with the powers of heaven and the peoples of the earth. No one can hold back his hand or say to him: 'What have you done?" In 2 Chr 20:6, Jehoshaphat says, "LORD, God of our ancestors, are you not the God who is in heaven? You rule over all the kingdoms of the nations. Power and might are in your hand, and no one can withstand you."

Fifth, God also gives political authority to governing rulers for the well-being of their subjects. For this reason, the apostle Paul commands everyone (literally, all souls) to obey ruling authorities in Rom 13:1–7. The governing authorities' use of judicial and police powers (the sword) constrains the expression of evil by its citizens. Every citizen has a vested interest in having governing authorities, for the absence of higher political authority produces anarchy. Societies without competent political authority provide opportunities for criminal gangs and other thuggish elements to seize local control for their ends, not for the well-being of the public at large. Because God mandates political authority, Paul commands believers to pray for those in authority in 1 Tim 2:1–2, whether or not they voted for those leaders (throughout history, few political leaders have ever been elected). If you find it difficult to pray for the political authorities over you, look around the world today where "failed states" exist and see how warlords and criminal gangs manage the affairs of those societies.

God sovereignly rules over the individual rulers of nations as well. Daniel 2, cited above, describes God setting up and deposing kings at his pleasure. Moreover, God may direct a king's heart to accomplish God's earthly purposes. Proverbs 21:1 says, "In the LORD's hand the king's heart is a stream of water that he channels toward all who please him." Though a pagan, King Nebuchadnezzar was considered a servant of God (Jer 25:9), doing God's bidding by defeating Judah and subjecting its citizens to Babylonian control. Isaiah prophesied that another pagan king, King Cyrus of Persia, would accomplish what God intended for him to bring an end to Babylonian rule. Isaiah 45:1–4 says,

> This is what the LORD says to his anointed, to Cyrus, whose right hand I take hold of to subdue nations before him and to strip kings of their armor, to open doors before him so that gates will not be shut: I will go before you and will level the mountains; I will break down gates of bronze and cut through bars of iron. I will give you hidden treasures, riches stored in secret places, so that you may know that I am the LORD, the God of Israel, who summons you by name. For the sake of Jacob my servant, of Israel my chosen, I

summon you by name and bestow on you a title of honor, though you do not acknowledge me.

Through the prophet Isaiah, God calls Cyrus "God's anointed" and selects him to release the Jews to go back to their homes in Palestine and to rebuild the temple of Jerusalem after their Babylonian captivity. Isaiah 44:28 says, "[Cyrus] is my shepherd and will accomplish all that I please; we will say of Jerusalem, 'Let it be rebuilt,' and of the temple, 'Let its foundations be laid.'" Ezra 1:1 shows the fulfillment of the prophecy: "In the first year of Cyrus king of Persia, in order to fulfill the word of the LORD spoken by Jeremiah, the LORD moved the heart of Cyrus king of Persia to make a proclamation throughout his realm and to put it in writing" (see also 2 Chr 36:22–23.)

God seems to care far less about the ideology of ruling regimes than we do. Rather, he seems to care about whether rulers shepherd their people and remain humble about their accomplishments. People in the Ancient Near East expected their kings to accomplish three things by their rule: (1) to militarily protect against foreign threats, (2) to judicially protect against internal threats, and (3) to spiritually protect against the whims of the gods by constructing temples and promoting worship.[26] God prescribed a kingship charter that exceeded those expectations, though it included the first two. In Deut 17:14–20, the king is instructed to constrain self-interest and the accumulation of wealth and wives, embody the righteousness of Jehovah, and, like God, be a shepherd of God's people (Ps 23, Ezek 34).

God sovereignly moves peoples' choices within nations, perhaps more often than we know. The Scriptures depict this most clearly with the Egyptians before the Exodus. In Exod 3:21, God proclaims, "And I will make the Egyptians favorably disposed toward this people, so that when you leave you will not go empty-handed." After disciplining the Egyptians with plagues, God moved them to fulfill his will. Exodus 12:33, says, "The Egyptians urged the people to hurry and leave the country. 'For otherwise,' they said, 'we will all die.'"

Sixth, God sovereignly rules over individual human beings. God ordains the length of our lives. Psalm 139:16 says: "Your eyes saw my unformed body. All the days ordained for me were written in your book before one of them came to be." He sovereignly rules over our death, poverty, and wealth. First Samuel 2:6–7 states, "The LORD brings death and makes alive; he brings down to the grave and raises up. The Lord sends poverty and wealth; he humbles and exalts." We cannot comprehend his intimate knowledge of

---

26. See Block, "Is Trump Our Cyrus?"

us. Psalm 139:1–5 says, "You have searched me, LORD, and you know me. You know when I sit and when I rise; you perceive my thoughts from afar. You discern my going out and my lying down; you are familiar with all my ways. Before a word is on my tongue, LORD, you know it completely. You hem me in behind and before, and you lay your hand upon me." God hems us in, constraining us individually for his purposes. King David marveled at the breadth of God's knowledge, wisdom, and power compared to human understanding. He says in Ps 8:3–4, "When I consider your heavens, the work of your fingers, the moon and the stars, which you have set in place, what is mankind that you are mindful of them, human beings that you care for them?" God mindfully thinks of us.

Individually, we are constrained by God's sovereign control of all the levels above us. God's purposes in his kingdom constrain us; his creation constrains us; international politics constrains us. The nation into which and leadership under which we are born constrain us. Were this a sociological essay, I would add that there would also be constraints from our culture and our families. In all this, God remains sovereign; he decides and acts in ways that support his kingdom's purposes and decides justly and truly. But in addition to all of this, God seemingly created some invariant laws of human behavior we humans frequently try to get around while avoiding the consequences of violating those laws.

At a minimum, God provides humans with rational minds that can link cause and effect, detect truth, and see correlations. Our logical minds were initially given to us as part of our creation in the image of God, the *imago dei*, to help build God's dominion on earth. With the ability to reason, we can make inferences, such as when we view creation and infer there must be a powerful and good creator (Rom 1:19–20). We can also understand human nature and the role and purpose of moral laws, which enhance the human and social condition. Political philosophers and church leaders have regarded these as natural laws (Rom 2:14), common-sense laws people have inferred from studying how human societies work best.

In the book of Romans, Paul outlines what happens to believers and unbelievers who violate the laws of rationality. In Rom 1:18–32, Paul shows the trajectory of unbelievers toward increasingly irrational thinking as they pursue unrighteousness to suppress the known truth of God revealed in nature and their conscience. God is not the Eye of Sauron of *The Lord of the Rings*, unblinkingly staring at each person, waiting to harm him or her;[27]

---

27. See, for example, Jackson, *Lord of the Rings*.

instead, the wrath of God is expressed through their increasingly irrational thinking and behavior, almost a law of "soul physics" for human beings. God expresses wrath through the consequence of increasing irrationality for those who suppress the truth in the pursuit of unrighteousness, just as it could be said God expresses his wrath on those who violate a fundamental law of physics like gravity by trying to step out into thin air believing they may avoid the consequence of falling downward.

Believers, on the other hand, face a different problem. Paul shows in Rom 2:1–16 that in attempting to follow the call of righteousness, believers will frequently fail to remain humble about their ability and about their desire to obey God. They will condemn those who fail to live up to God's law while enjoying sin, even secretly in their hearts. Believers irrationally believe they are qualified to judge others outside of the faith when they have been given, by the grace of God, both the desire and the ability to follow his norms for human behavior. This results in legalism, which blinds the believer to the truth just as unbelief blinds unbelievers who pursue unrighteousness. The believer should never insert himself between God and the nonbeliever through personal judgment. That is above our "pay grade."

There also are laws of reciprocity among humans. One is the law of "sowing and reaping" (see Prov 11:2, Luke 6:38, Gal 6:7, and 2 Cor 9:6). How we treat others will frequently be reciprocated by others in how they treat us. How we invest in others will be reciprocated. Jesus makes the case for this law with both its negative and positive consequences. For the negative, in Matt 7:1–6, Jesus teaches us that to judge or condemn another will result in condemnation coming back on us in full. There is a stark reality to the norm Jesus lays down; he says, "Do not judge, or you too will be judged." Then he adds more detail—the reality of the human condition, an admission that we will judge others: "For in the same way you judge others, you will be judged, and with the measure you use, it will be measured to you." We will judge, and we will do it all the time. It's an essential human brain/mind tool to evaluate oneself, one's peers, and one's circumstances. But we must consider the measure, or the standards, by which we judge. Our judgment should never condemn another with no final appeal (for that's what judgment means); we will never know the other human heart or all the facts behind their words or actions. Just as importantly, Jesus points out that when we judge others, we tend to avoid evaluating our hearts, for we have likely thought or committed the very sins and failures we presume to see in others.

Positively, Jesus encourages his followers to pursue a new, better principle for human interaction. This better principle remains normative for our time on earth and will likely describe our behavior in the new heavens and earth, so now is the time to practice it. In Matt 7:12, he says: "So in everything, do to others what you would have them do to you, for this sums up the Law and the Prophets." Do you want others to think kindly of your intentions? Do you want people to avoid making unwarranted assumptions about what you are saying and doing? Jesus wants us to habituate ourselves to think kindly of others first. Give people the benefit of the doubt when you see something that seems odd or out of place. Check with a person to find out their reasoning before inferring ulterior motives. Would the church consistently manifest a community of people who lived by this norm. If this were descriptive of our behavior in society at large and not just normative for believers, the mainstream media and our social media, let alone our civil society, would look vastly different today.

While we are hemmed, or constrained, by God, he allows us to choose to follow him or follow our folly. The Western mindset often overestimates the importance of free will. As we've seen, there's a great deal over which we have no control. The Scriptures tell us we need God's help to incline our hearts (Ps 119:36–40), even as we incline our ears to wisdom and apply our hearts to his words (Prov 2). There is, therefore, a balance between divine sovereignty and human responsibility.

Daniel lived in that balance.

DANIEL AND GOD'S SOVEREIGNTY

How might Daniel have conceived of God's sovereignty in his own life? Remember that by about age fifteen, Daniel was forcibly taken captive out of his homeland and marched by military convoy to Babylon, with only his three friends as companions. Babylon likely took captives from Egypt and the surrounding provinces of Palestine outside of Judah, so Daniel would have been among a variety of people, probably with few who were friendly to him. Once in Babylon, he was likely castrated as part of the court rituals of the Near East at the time and given a pagan name, further distancing him from his ethnic identity and rendering him incapable of meeting the requirements of a righteous Jew. What did Daniel think about all of this?

Scripture does not tell us, but perhaps for good reasons. By not describing how Daniel reasoned through the challenges and dealt with his situation, the book allows us to put ourselves in his place and work out our understanding of God's sovereignty in our lives.

Daniel likely saw that the different levels of God's sovereign created ruling around everyone provided at least three things: constraints, resources, and opportunities. The constraints of the various levels of God's sovereign rule presented themselves obviously to Daniel. He did not choose to be born into a particular family, nation, time in history, or with the international politics of his day. He did not select the economic conditions of his day. He did not voluntarily choose to serve the pagan country of Babylon. He knew that no one could escape God's purposes in his kingdom or be reborn into a different family or genetic inheritance.[28] He, like we, must learn and grow within our given constraints.

Beyond constraints, God provided manifold, though finite, resources for Daniel's life. Such resources would include baseline intellectual capacities (for academics or skills in administration) and his genetic inheritance (for physical capability and beauty). Daniel's God-given resources would also include his family's wealth or poverty, though this ceased to help him once he became a captive. Daniel's resources were stewarded and increased through his diligence in understanding Scripture and God's design for him as a believer. At times, Daniel may have thought God seemed remote from him. It's something most believers experience in their lives. But, by his persistent study of God's word and prayer, he learned to trust God's sovereign direction not only for his own life but also for the lives and destiny of his fellow Jews and their nation, as well as the nations around him. Daniel learned to avoid worrying over things he could not control. In addition to not worrying about where he would get his next meal, Daniel worried little about the political direction of his country and other countries, except insofar as they followed God's law or failed to follow it (Dan 9:4–17). He concerned himself with how he, his friends, fellow Jews, and the various kings he served responded to God.

Opportunities differ from constraints. From any person's perspective, opportunities may appear random. Such opportunities are what theologians would call providence, where God provides for his loyal followers and sometimes those who don't follow him. For Daniel, his opportunities came from the very constraints of his captivity. Daniel had readied himself for God's providential actions in Babylon by his earlier spiritual preparations.

---

28. There is some evidence that we can neurologically escape our genetic constraints, within limits, with new genetic expressions. See Rana, "Epigenetics."

GOD'S SOVEREIGN RULE WITH DANIEL IN BABYLON

As we'll see in the following chapters, opportunities grow with such diligence in preparation. In 1 Pet 3:15, Peter commands us to revere Christ as Lord of our lives and prepare to give reasons for the hope in us, stating that God will bring along many opportunities to share our faith in ways we never thought possible.[29] Peter offers sound advice for life: constantly prepare yourself spiritually and in your areas of interest. God will sovereignly provide opportunities to use you for God's kingdom throughout your life.

Daniel ably deals with God's sovereignty during his day. Isaiah and Jeremiah had prophesied that Judah would be disciplined for disobeying God. For the faithful Jews paying attention to such prophecies, Babylon's rise in the late seventh century should have come as no surprise. Some one hundred years before Isaiah had prophesied (Isa 39:5–7) that some of Hezekiah's descendants would be taken to Babylon and made eunuchs in the Babylonian court; there seems to be little chance that Daniel could have known that he would have been one of those captives. Still, he would have been alert to Babylon's rise. Daniel and his friends were utterly constrained by both the national and international politics of the day and God's sovereign control over the destinies of those nations. Yet, within these constraints, there were opportunities for Daniel and his friends.

Somehow, he and his three friends were able to overcome the trauma of forced migration to Babylon and subsequent castration. We do not know how he and his friends did so, but we've identified some ways it may have occurred. Once they were taken by force and the prophecy of captivity became very real and personal, he and his friends may have realized the importance of the prophecy of Isa 49:6, which directed them to take agency in their roles as God's servants. Knowing that he had a role in God's kingdom seems consistent with what we see with the rest of Daniel's life—a life set apart for God through his excellence at work, faithfulness to God, and obedience to political authority. Everyone Daniel worked with or for acknowledged that he served the living God. In Dan 9, we will see that he initiates a prayer for repentance that brings about God's promise to return the Jews to their ancestral homeland. We also see that in addition to his God-given intelligence, Daniel was given the resource of wisdom in all manner of things that would pertain to his newfound administrative career, a career that he could never have expected.

As Daniel and his friends were likely raised as religious Jews, they would have been aware of the need to obey their parents and all authority.

---

29. For many examples, see Hugh Ross and Kathy Ross, *Ready*.

Scripture teaches that disobeying authority equates to a form of idolatry and divination (1 Sam 15:23). Knowing that God had ordained the events of their day, Daniel and his friends would have been aware of the Scriptures that speak highly of hard work and diligence and obeying authority, including political authority. Proverbs 12:11 and 14:23 expressly talk about the need to work well. Ecclesiastes 9:10 says, "Whatever your hand finds to do, do it with all your might." And Prov 16:3 says, "Commit to the Lord whatever you do, and he will establish your plans." First Corinthians 10:31 evokes the same idea: "So whether you eat or drink or whatever you do, do it all for the glory of God." We give God glory by honoring him with our excellent and diligent work, whatever that work might be. The believer's work ethic should accurately represent God's righteousness, faithfulness, and excellence. As Jesus says in Matt 5:16 in the Sermon on the Mount, we are to let our "light shine before others, that they may see your good deeds and glorify your Father in heaven."

While we work for those who employ us, we fundamentally work for God. Daniel exemplified hard work in his years of service as if he was serving God and not man. Colossians 3:23-24 says, "Whatever you do, work at it with all your heart, as working for the Lord, not for human masters, since you know that you will receive an inheritance from the Lord as a reward." Daniel seemed to know that even though he was under political authority, and was not much more than a court servant when he first started, he was working for an eternal reward (see Dan 12:13). After years of faithfulness to God, and diligence and excellence in his work, he was told that he was considered "highly esteemed" in the kingdom of God (Dan 10:11). His faithfulness in all these things led his acts to be included in the roll call of the faithful deeds of those who lived for God and not for men found in Heb 11.

Daniel models how to think about God's sovereignty in a fallen world. Though constrained by events beyond his control, he dedicated his life to God. He clearly understood that the fear of the Lord was the beginning of wisdom (Prov 1:7). While he was gifted with many capacities, Daniel worked hard on his studies and improved his skills for navigating his way through life. (Proverbs 2:1–15 gives the many benefits of a diligent pursuit of wisdom.) As we study his first appeal in Dan 1, we will see that he was very adept at learning, and he and his friends excelled at gaining knowledge of political administration at the hands of the Babylonian court; in fact, they were found many times superior to the others taken for court service.

Daniel lived a life of integrity by integrating both the spiritual and the physical. He excelled at both. He could do this knowing that God remained sovereignly in control over God's kingdom, the physical creation, the destiny of nations, and Daniel's own life. Daniel succeeded by subordinating the activities of his daily life to God's kingdom purposes.

4

Daniel's First Appeal: More Vegetables

THE FIRST CHAPTER OF Daniel is set during the initial phase of captivity for Daniel and his three friends. The text begins by giving the reader a timestamp of when the events occur—that is, in the third year of the reign of Jehoiakim, king of Judah (605 BC). This ties the events to the Babylonian conquest of Egypt at Carchemish that year. Though Babylon primarily wanted to eliminate Egypt's support for the Assyrian Empire and Assyria's control over the area of Palestine and Syria, the spoils of war allowed Babylon to take booty and people from the more minor powers in the region, such as Syrians, Phoenicians, Egyptians, and Judeans.[1]

The story unfolds dramatically as Daniel makes his first appeal after suffering the trauma of being taken captive and separated from his family, marched some nine hundred miles, stripped of his ethnic identity, and likely emasculated. He and his friends will be given new names, enrolled into the "master's program" of Babylonian administration for three years, and feted with the king's choice food from the royal court. Daniel 1:3–7 gives us the context:

> Then the king ordered Ashpenaz, chief of his court officials, to bring in some of the Israelites from the royal family and the nobility—young men without any physical defect, handsome, showing aptitude for every kind of learning, well informed, quick to understand, and qualified to serve in the king's palace. He was to teach them the language and literature of the Babylonians. The king assigned them a daily amount of food and wine from the king's table.

1. Bryce, *Babylonia*, 76.

DANIEL'S FIRST APPEAL: MORE VEGETABLES

> They were to be trained for three years, and after that they were to enter the king's service. Among these were some from Judah: Daniel, Hananiah, Mishael and Azariah. The chief official gave them new names: to Daniel, the name Belteshazzar; to Hananiah, Shadrach; to Mishael, Meschach; and to Azariah, Abednego.

Ashpenaz, the chief of the eunuchs, gave these four Jews new, pagan names for formal adoption into the empire. For millennia, empires have changed the names of conquered people to assimilate them into their cultures and customs. The Babylonians used many methods to encourage social and religious conformity of newly conquered people or, in this case, the select few taken from various countries to serve in the court of Babylon.[2] Here, giving new, culturally, and religiously significant names would be one way to apply social pressure on these young men. The new names are listed below with their assumed meanings:[3]

Table 3: Names	
Hebrew name/meaning	Pagan name/likely meaning
Daniel: "God is my judge"	Belteshazzar: "Bel (Marduk) protect his life" (Marduk, chief god of Babylon)
Hananiah: "The Lord shows grace"	Shaddrach: "command of Aku" after a Sumerian moon-god
Mishael: "Who is what God is"	Meshach: "Who is what Aku is"
Azariah: "The Lord helps"	Abednego: servant of Nego/Nebo (i.e., Nabu)

Daniel 1:8–14 gives us more information:

> But Daniel resolved not to defile himself with the royal food and wine, and he asked the chief official for permission not to defile himself this way. Now God had caused the official to show favor and sympathy to Daniel, but the official told Daniel, "I am afraid of my lord the king, who has assigned your food and drink. Why should he see you looking worse than the other young men your age? The king would then have my head because of you." Daniel then said to the guard whom the chief official had appointed over Daniel, Hananiah, Mishael and Azariah, "Please test your servants for ten days: Give us nothing but vegetables to eat and water to drink. Then compare our appearance with that of the young men

---

2. Kelman, "Compliance," 51–60.
3. Barker et. al., *NIV Study Bible*, 1300.

who eat the royal food, and treat your servants in accordance with what you see." So he agreed to this and tested them for ten days.

Daniel's treatment at the hands of the Babylonians would have been against his will. Still, he selects a way to keep some social and religious boundary, or separation, from the other captives and the Babylonian religious and social customs by requesting a different diet. Yet the reasons why Daniel chose to make an appeal regarding the food remain contested. Most commentators say that Daniel decided to take a stand over the king's choice of food because it was used in pagan sacrificial rites. Many commentators seem to assume that the Babylonians used meat in pagan sacrifices.[4] Daniel's objection to the food because of this use is a reasonable inference from New Testament passages such as 1 Cor 8, where Paul talks about how pagan converts to Christianity were concerned about eating meat sacrificed to idols in the pagan practices of Greece. I wonder, however, whether commentators use the New Testament to read into the Old Testament without considering a few other facts.

Daniel never says the food they were to be given was sacrificed to pagan gods. Some historical records from the Seleucid period indicate that the king's choice food was first sacrificed to the gods.[5] Leftovers, which were plenty, were then distributed to the king and his court. More to the point, Daniel eats meat and drinks wine later in life (Dan 10:2), so he may have appealed for a temporary, albeit necessary, expedient.

Daniel may have appealed for two reasons. The first would be to respect the dietary laws of Israel by avoiding proscribed foods if Babylon served them; the second would be out of an abundance of caution about Babylonian social pressure. He likely avoided eating proscribed meat for the first reason and drinking wine for the second reason. These reasons may need to be clarified to contemporary, Western, and non-Jewish readers.

First, though he would be living in a foreign land, Daniel would have wanted to adhere to Levitical laws. Such laws specified the types of meat that were allowable for a religious Jew to eat and other kinds that could not be eaten (see Lev 11; Exod 23:19, 34:26). Pig meat would have been anathema to a religious Jew. Those laws also forbid a religious Israelite to eat even acceptable meat with its blood or cooked with milk. We do not have written records of what the Jewish religious community in exile thought about the procedures for ensuring adherence to the law. They begin writing

4. *ESV Study Bible*, 1586–87; see also Barker et al., *NIV Study Bible*, 1300.
5. Oates, *Babylon*, 175.

procedures down only much later in the Babylonian and Jerusalem Talmud. Those procedures later came to be called kosher and koshering. Wine, on the other hand, was not restricted by Levitical law.

The Babylonians, however, had no such restrictions—or at least none that we see from the available scribal texts.[6] It seems likely that Daniel would want to avoid eating meat until he was in a position to make sure it was processed following Levitical laws, and that position would only come later in his career when he was not beholden to the strict procedures during his training program. Further, until more Jews were forced into exile in Babylon, there would not have been a large enough community of like-minded people to help ensure the process remained pure.

Second, and maybe more importantly, Babylonian practices were designed to socialize new immigrants into their religious, cultural, and political system. The process of enculturation began when the Babylonians compelled him to come to Babylon without his consent, gave him a pagan name, and likely emasculated him. Nowhere do we see Daniel resist any of these things; he would likely have been immediately killed by his overseers for such defiance. These things would have put enormous social pressure on Daniel to conform to Babylonian culture and religious practices and begin acculturating to Babylonian values. Giving Daniel a pagan name and feeding him the king's food would have been done to honor him and elicit his loyalty. Notice the push of the constraints imposed on him and then the pull of the fine meats and wine he would be given—the trappings of social prestige.

In addition to meat, typically unavailable to the average Babylonian, wine was imported and likely only available to the rich and the king's court members. Wine was not prohibited in dietary law (Deut 8:8), but both meat and wine would have been symbols of high status in Babylonian society. In the context of family and convivial company, wine used in moderation can promote health, enhance social acceptance, and lessen personal inhibitions.

Yet Daniel wanted to stay a Jew and to stay faithful to God. Daniel was also young and vulnerable. The young have a more challenging time resisting pressure for social conformity.[7] And he recognized something that we in the modern world can miss: eating and socializing with people indicates acceptance of their society and social norms; this was true in the ancient world and is true in many places worldwide today. As one scholar noted,

6. Oates, *Babylon*, 177.
7. Pasupathi, "Age Differences," 170–74.

"Eating at the same table (1 Sam 20:30–34; 2 Sam 9:9–13) or providing food from one's portion (Gen 43:34) signifies both an honor conferred and an expectation of loyalty."[8]

He may have recognized that he would be separated from the rest of the young candidates for the training program by avoiding wine and meat and consuming only vegetables and water. He would be "set apart" to fulfill God's kingdom purposes for his day, as recorded in Isa 49:6. But rather than speaking brashly, Daniel appeals with humility and grace.

THE APPEAL

Several things stand out about Daniel's appeal. First, he crafted his appeal so that his political overseer could decide Daniel's fate, as it were. Daniel asked and didn't demand that his superior accede to his request; instead, he offered Ashpenaz a viable alternative and allowed him to determine after ten days whether that alternative was satisfactory and could continue. Second, because he provided an alternative, Daniel implicitly acknowledged Ashpenaz's real fear that, should Daniel and his friends lose too much weight and appear unfit for the king's service, Ashpenaz could lose his life by considering Daniel's request. Third, Daniel respected Ashpenaz's authority by requesting permission to make an alternative.

Daniel never acted or spoke impetuously. We see him quietly determined to prepare for contingencies; it seems reasonable to believe Daniel prepared throughout his life for the unexpected challenges he would face in Babylon. His parents likely raised him as a religious Jew, and he would have been no stranger to the writings in the Mosaic law and the prophets, including Isaiah. Isaiah had prophesied that Assyria would be God's agent to discipline Israel (Isa 7:18–20), prophecies given nearly one hundred years before. Isaiah prophesied that Cyrus of Persia would be used to deliver Jews from Babylonian captivity (Isa 44:28—45:1), an event yet in the future for Daniel. Then, there were those prophets who were active just before the arrival of Babylonian armies: Jeremiah and Habakkuk. They spoke of the discipline God would impose on Judah for failing to repent of its wickedness and turn toward him. They also spoke with foreshadow of Babylon as the nation that would bring about God's discipline. In Jer 25:7–11, the prophet identified the king of Babylon, Nebuchadnezzar, as his servant in carrying out God's mandate of judgment.

8. Newsom, *Commentary*, 106–7.

Habakkuk recoiled at both Judah's wickedness and even more so at the wicked nation, Babylon, which God would use to bring about Judah's discipline. In a series of complaints and responses, Habakkuk cries against Judah's wickedness (Hab 1:2–4), and God answers that Babylon would be God's agent to discipline Judah (vv. 5–11). Habakkuk complains that God would use such an evil nation (1:12—2:1) against one more righteous. Still, God answers that Babylon will eventually be punished and that faithful living during that time will be rewarded (2:2–20). God tells the faithful to wait (2:3) for God's judgment to come upon Babylon. In his letter to the exiles in Babylon, Jeremiah goes further. He says to them that they are to "seek the peace and prosperity of the city to which I have carried you into exile. Pray to the LORD for it, because if it prospers, you too will prosper" (Jer 29:7). After reviewing God's historical acts of judgment and deliverance, Habakkuk finally concludes that he will wait on God's sovereign moves in judgment on Babylon (Hab 3:15–20). These prophets illustrated how Daniel and his friends may have considered serving in its court.

During his trip to Babylon, Daniel likely spent much time with his three friends in prayer, study, and fellowship. We infer this by working backward from what we see in the book of Daniel later. We certainly see in the book of Daniel that they worked well together on several things. In Dan 1:12, even though Daniel appeals, they had agreed to let Daniel speak for all of them in his request not to eat the meat or drink the wine of the king's table, as Daniel asks the guard in charge of him to "test your servants" for several days. In Dan 2:17–18, Daniel and his three friends pray together over Daniel's ability to interpret the king's dream, which, against the odds, he can do, saving his own life and the lives of his friends, as well as all of the court shamans. Once he successfully recalled and interpreted the dream, Daniel requested that his three friends receive promotions as part of the rewards Nebuchadnezzar offered Daniel. The king granted Daniel's wishes. Daniel's friends were ready for a promotion, as was Daniel. Either Daniel had already secured their consent, or their relationship was so well ordered that he could freely ask the king on their behalf.

We also see that in the middle of this "test," Daniel "resolved not to defile himself" (Dan 1:8). Daniel and perhaps his friends, likely with prayer and fasting, petitioned God for an approach that could allow them to remain "set apart" for his kingdom's purposes. Earnest resolutions for kingdom purposes are only enabled by seeking God's sovereign purposes. We wait and resolve to stand ready to act as God directs, and in the manner he directs, into a path or future that often surprises us. Daniel's resolve to avoid defilement seems similar to the resolution it takes to seek God's wisdom from above, of which Daniel had plenty. Psalm 1:7 says, "The fear of the Lord is the beginning of knowledge, but fools despise wisdom and instruction." But King Solomon warns that acquiring it requires drive and intentionality. In Prov 2:1–6, through a series of conditionals, the king warns what it will take to obtain first, the fear of the Lord, and second, the wisdom he gives: "My son, *if* you accept my words and store up my commands within you, turning your ear to wisdom and applying your heart to understanding—indeed *if* you call out for insight and cry aloud for understanding, *and if* you look for it as for silver and search for it as for hidden treasure, *then* you will understand the fear of the Lord and find the knowledge of God. For the Lord gives wisdom, and from his mouth come knowledge and understanding" (emphasis added). James 1:5 says, "If any of you lacks wisdom, he should ask God who gives generously to all without finding fault, and it will be given to you."

Notice, too, that Dan 1:9 says, "Now God had caused the official to show favor and sympathy to Daniel." Have you ever requested that of God—for him to cause those over you to show favor and compassion to you? The text doesn't say Daniel made that request, but he may have made it during his prayer. He certainly contributed to receiving the favor and compassion of Babylonian authorities by having already committed to God's kingdom purposes for his day. He was utterly incapable of accomplishing this alone, as are we. Daniel, in his weakness, let God work through him, and God must be involved in and through our weakness. At the very least, Daniel contributed to the Babylonian authorities' favorable view of him by establishing a good relationship with his supervisors, obedience to their authority, and discipline in his work. Without that obedience, discipline, and relationship, it is unlikely he would have gotten an audience with Ashpenaz to appeal.

Several other features of Daniel's appeal suggest a great deal of preparation for it. First, he didn't reject serving in the king's court, which would likely have cost him his life. As committed followers of Christ, we often must determine where and when to take our stand. Daniel sensed that it wasn't there at those points where the Babylonians had absolute control. This is Daniel's wisdom. Second, Daniel never displays any anger, bitterness, or revenge toward the Babylonian authorities that stripped him of his family, homeland, religion, and likely his ability to sire offspring. We discussed

DANIEL'S FIRST APPEAL: MORE VEGETABLES

earlier how Daniel may have learned to cope with the trauma he undoubtedly suffered at the hands of the Babylonians. While God may have supernaturally graced Daniel with deliverance from such haunting thoughts and feelings, it seems more likely that the process he went through helped him recover before making this appeal. Third, Daniel decided to make this appeal in concert with his three friends, which suggests a great deal of deliberate coordination on their part, and, thus, the strength of supportive friends.

Daniel makes no demands of his superiors. Instead, he prayerfully and thoughtfully offers a genuine alternative to the king's orders to the chief official. He determined that he needed to avoid defiling himself, whether because the food itself could pollute him or because he determined that requesting a vegetable diet alone could help him and his friends be "set apart" from the other captives entering the king's service, or perhaps both at the same time. Was the king's order for those entering his service intended to shame and pollute those entering his service? This seems unlikely, as he would be polluting everyone in his service. Instead, the Babylonian court offers the choicest food and drink, not generally available to the average Babylonian, to ensure the health and success of those entering the king's service and to confer some "status" on his servants. The king wants people to succeed in gaining help to administer the empire. Daniel's alternative would accomplish the objectives of the king's order to make the servants healthy. In fact, at the end of the trial period of ten days, they were said to "look healthier and better nourished" (1:15) than the others (the King James version says, "fairer and fatter").

The appeal Daniel makes also allows his alternative to be tested publicly. Daniel believed God would sovereignly help him in this test, and his dependence on God was demonstrable. He now puts his trust in the sovereign God to the test, not in rebellion to political control but in reliance on God alone. The test was not subjective either. He didn't ask Ashpenaz how he would feel about it. He encouraged him to see whether the alternative Daniel proposed worked and evaluate the results by comparing Daniel and his three friends against the others in the king's service.

Finally, Daniel appeals in such a way in order to ease the fear of the chief official. Daniel likely respected the commander of the eunuchs personally, as well as respecting his position professionally. He understood that the king expected complete obedience from his servants. Failure to carry out the king's orders would likely result in his execution. By easing the official's fear he would fail to carry out the king's orders, Daniel's appeal accomplishes his own purpose and the king's and, by implication, Ashpenaz's.

From these observations about his request, we can infer that Daniel made a righteous appeal appealingly and righteously.

Daniel consistently displays respectful obedience to political authority, and he never criticizes the unrighteous practices of the Babylonians. Their practices were outlawed for Israel in the Mosaic law (Exod 22:17), yet Daniel doesn't shame the shamans whom he surely knew worshipped wooden idols that could not speak and practiced a profession that offered no lasting value. While the Babylonians were famous for developing astronomy, it remained subordinate to their astrology. The whole cadre of magicians, astrologers, enchanters, and sorcerers was a caste of professional religious people who did everything from reading the livers of dead animals to anticipating success or failure on the battlefield to reading the omens of human lives from the position of stars. They also included magic. Historian Will Durant explains some of these practices:

> Magic formulas for the elimination of demons, the avoidance of evil and the prevision of the future constitute the largest category in the Babylonian writings found in the library of Ashurbanipal. Some of the tablets are manuals of astrology; others are lists of omens celestial and terrestrial, with expert advice for reading them; others are treatises on the interpretation of dreams, rivaling in their ingenious incredibility the most advanced products of modern psychology; still others offer instruction in divining the future by examining the entrails of animals, or by observing the form and position of a drop of oil let fall into a jar of water. Hepatoscopy—observation of the liver of animals—was a favorite method of divination among the Babylonian priests, and passed from them into the classical world; for the liver was believed to be the seat of the mind in both animals and men. No king would undertake a campaign or advance to a battle, no Babylonian would risk a crucial decision or begin an enterprise of great moment, without employing a priest or a soothsayer to read the omens for him in one or another of these recondite ways.[9]

These people were the king's advisors because in Babylonian society, religion, administration, art, and warfare were intermingled and subordinated to their religious worldview to a degree we cannot imagine today.

---

9. Durant, *Civilization*, 243–44.

DANIEL'S FIRST APPEAL: MORE VEGETABLES

Ancient political and military leaders throughout the Near East relied on these advisors for all significant decisions. This was true for Assyrians no less than Babylonians, Persians, Greeks, and, later, the Romans, and probably others. They relied on their readings of events, particularly war decisions. The decision to go to war was particularly fraught with uncertainty, and "given the uncertainty of war in general, ancient military commanders made considerable use of divination, looking to the gods to provide information that human resources could not. As a result, good *manteis* (seers), which means men who could not only correctly advise on the outcome of future actions, but who also had a record of being on the victorious side, were highly valued, and could expect rich rewards from the individuals and communities they served."[10] (The future will always remain a mystery. To ease the potential for bad outcomes, political leaders today use the modern version of this ancient practice: spies and intelligence.)

Perhaps Daniel pitied the Babylonians for their religious beliefs. Maybe he, like Paul at the Areopagus, understood that pagan religious beliefs, though of human origin, may reflect a more profound desire to connect with something more powerful than what life offered. He may have understood what Paul understood about the pagans of his era: they were not far from the gospel. They were certainly closer than modern materialists. Keep in mind that the ancient Babylonians, for all their relative wealth and material prosperity, lived in a fairly hostile physical world, and their religion reflected that dour view of life. One scholar paints the picture for us:

> The account of the great Babylonian festivals may give a wrong impression of the religion of which they were a particular expression, for it might suggest a people serene and joyful in the cultivation of their fertile land and the cult of their patron gods. But we must not forget the great quantity of magical and divinatory tests, with the ceaseless and always uncertain effort to foresee and influence the dreaded course of fate, the ills which threaten all existence. We must bear in mind the dismal prospect of a squalid life beyond the tomb, when the soul will wander wearily in search of remembrance. For the Babylonians, like the Sumerians, believe in life after death, but, as with the Sumerians, this belief is not associated with any views on retribution for the good and evil deeds of this life. The abode of the dead is situated beneath the earth

---

10. Bowden, *Alexander*, 39–40.

and is enveloped in darkness. Its inhabitants drag out a wretched existence, eating dust and drinking dirty water.[11]

No wonder Daniel didn't shame them. He trusted God and knew he was fortunate to be alive and to be able to serve God while serving in the court of Babylon. Daniel could execute God's kingdom purposes in an alien political kingdom. Daniel didn't expect righteous behavior from people who didn't know God.

Finally, Daniel diligently applied himself to his studies. Early in the appeal, the Babylonian court looked for several things for its recruits into the king's service. They had to be "young men without any physical defect, handsome, showing aptitude for every kind of learning, well informed, quick to understand, and qualified to serve in the king's palace" (Dan 1:4). In addition to being perfect physical specimens and objectively handsome by the culture's standards, the promising recruits had to pass some tests to determine their intellectual aptitude for serving as an advisor in the king's court. Today, we use various measures to enter college, graduate, medical, or law schools, and even the military. What tests the Babylonians employed, we may never know. It seems likely that the candidates were asked a series of questions about what they understood of the world, how well they grasped instruction, and their potential to serve in various positions of administration. We know more about the language and the literature of the Babylonians than what tests they used to assess aptitude.

Babylonians preserved their predecessors' traditions, culture, religion, and languages for centuries. These peoples included the indigenous Sumerians and the Akkadians, a Semitic people who migrated in later. Chaldeans, another Western Semitic people, began populating Mesopotamia between the tenth and ninth centuries BC. These Chaldeans later made remarkable developments in astronomy and provided some of the leading political figures during the Babylonian captivity.

Some of the art on the gates of Babylon was in the Sumerian language. Later, the Akkadians developed cuneiform writing to record official documents on dried clay tablets and cylinders. While cuneiform may have been initially designed for commercial purposes, by the time of Daniel, it had become the official language for diplomacy, scholarship, and religion. It required several years of hard work to master.[12] During the mid-eighth century BC, the Assyrian Tiglath-Pileser III introduced Eastern Aramaic as

---

11. Moscati, *Face*, 74.
12. Kriwaczek, *Babylon*, 244, 264–65.

the *lingua franca* of the empire, which also became the common language of the Babylonians, who were subordinate to the Assyrian Empire. Eastern Aramaic, a common language throughout the region, differed from the Palestinian Aramaic of Judea, but even so, it was a relatively easy language to learn. So, Daniel and his friends had to learn the dialect of eastern Aramaic, Akkadian cuneiform, and likely Sumerian.

Learning languages takes a great deal of effort. The modern Defense Language Institute trains our military personnel in foreign languages and so may help guide us. A friend of mine studied in an intensive program for thirteen months to become fluent in Russian. While studying Russian, students will also study Russian culture, history, customs, and practices. At the end of the thirteen months of intensive training, students are tested on a 5-point scale for their proficiency (with 5 being "functionally native proficiency," the proficiency of a very well-educated native).[13] Typically, the military trains its students not so much to interact with others in their culture but to staff "listening" posts worldwide to understand what others are saying and thinking. After thirteen months of intensive training, my friend could interpret the Russian military language but was not fluent enough to speak Russian as a Russian native. He would likely have been rated four 4 to 5 in listening and 3 in conversation. Daniel and his friends likely became very proficient at being scribes with Sumerian and Cuneiform, and at least Daniel became fluent in Eastern Aramaic, also called Imperial Aramaic, for half of his book was written in it.

In addition to the literature and languages, our young friends likely also learned about administering an empire. Because Babylon sees little rain but sits astride the two great rivers, the Tigris and the Euphrates, the Babylonians kept detailed records of floods and irrigation. They also kept records on diplomacy and war. They also recorded their architectural achievements, especially under Nebuchadnezzar, who began a vast building campaign that astounded the ancient world.[14] Daniel and friends would likely have been required to acquaint themselves with this rich tradition.

But then they also had to learn Babylonian "science" and mathematics. As recently as 747 BC, the Chaldeans became more prominent in Babylon's political history when Nabonassa, a Chaldean, ascended the throne. By then, the Chaldeans had established highly accurate records of the times and motions of the stars, so much so that they began to keep very accurate

---

13. See Defense Language Institute, "Language Proficiency Assessment."
14. Oates, *Babylon*, 128.

records for the various lines of kings. Later, the Greeks based their early astronomy on the Chaldean understanding. Astronomy depended heavily upon learning mathematics.[15] All of their "science," however, was subordinate to their religious understanding. It has been said that the Chaldeans, in particular, and Babylonians, in general, looked at the world to discover how things worked with religious undertones. In their records of the motions of the stars and the seasons, they also included detailed lists of floods, plagues, diseases, and other things. They also began to accumulate detailed descriptions of what animal activities meant for them—for example, what might happen when a dog peered into the temple or sat down by a king and what those actions portended for the future. It's almost impossible to know what Daniel thought about Babylonian religion because it was so intimately tied up with the Babylonian understanding of the world, politics, and administration. Yet we know he and his friends remained faithful to God while studying and gaining mastery over the beneficial things of their education.

These young men worked extremely hard at their studies. They were at a ripe age, too, for modern neuroscience shows that from age twelve to twenty-four is when the adolescent brain is pruning (sloughing off neurons) and growing new ones at an accelerated rate in preparation for the rest of life.[16] The brain at that age undergoes a radical and rapid transformation. Their diligent studying paid off. At the end of their three-year graduate program in Babylonian administration, our friends passed with more than flying colors. According to the text, when Nebuchadnezzar or an appointed servant evaluated them, they were found an order of magnitude better than the magicians and the enchanters (1:20). God certainly equipped them, for we see in v. 17, "To these four young men God gave knowledge and understanding of all kinds of literature and learning." This is where God and humans intersect when, by diligent obedience to him, God honors those who excel in the tasks he gives them.

At this young age, Daniel presented his appeal with less ego and more expertise than most of us do most of the time. Would that we practiced this conversational strategy with others in our day-to-day living. By seeking permission from Ashpenaz, Daniel says something assertive and disarming simultaneously. He asserts his needs while respecting the needs of the other—in this case, the chief of eunuchs. Further, he does not say the Babylonians will defile him; he says he does not want to defile himself with the

---

15. Oates, *Babylon*, 113.
16. Siegel, *Brainstorm*, 73–100.

king's food choice. The onus is taken off Ashpenaz and is now on Daniel; his approach likely caused Ashpenaz to ask why the food may be defiling to Daniel, though the text does not record this. Daniel likely took time to explain how the food would have defiled him and his three friends. In the process, he let him know that he would not eat the king's choice of food assertively but peacefully.

Daniel expertly phrased his appeal in another way. He never demanded success, nor did he demand changes in others. He lets Ashpenaz determine whether the diet worked. Of course, what Daniel writes intrigues us further because, after talking to Ashpenaz, Daniel submits the proposal to the guard Ashpenaz had appointed over Daniel and his friends. The guard was likely given guidance to allow Daniel's proposed diet and that the guard may evaluate the results. We do not know whether the guard or Ashpenaz kept the extra portions of the king's rations for themselves, which indeed would have been a temptation for either or both.

Daniel submitted to the legitimate political authority of Babylonian officials throughout this process. While he determined that the best way to remain "set apart" for God's kingdom purposes in Babylon was to appeal for a restrictive diet, he remained under the authority of the king's men. He appeals in such a way as to get the commander to accede to his request without demanding changes in others. Daniel determined that he would not defile himself, so it's also true that he likely would have been willing to die for his request. And that should cause us to pause and reflect on how important the request was to Daniel. Daniel wanted to have some separation from the political society but not a separation that would shame members of that society. At the same time, it seems likely that Daniel wouldn't hold a grudge against anyone in political authority should the appeal fail. Daniel refused to live with anger and bitterness toward the Babylonians despite all they had done to him.

My thesis is that Daniel led an exemplary life of faith during historic political events because he had committed to God's kingdom purposes for his day. Because he had, Daniel's behavior throughout this first appeal should encourage us to follow his example. He navigated the dilemma that was imposed on him. Daniel's dilemma is our dilemma today: how to obey political authority while avoiding becoming absorbed by the political order in which we find ourselves. As we have seen, God established political authority after the fall to restrain evil expression in society. Without it, societies can descend into anarchy or allow for the rise of tyranny, so we are obliged to remain obedient and even pray for those in power.

However, political authority is a concession to human sin. It is essential, but not supremely important, to the believer. God's kingdom and his purposes will always supersede human political systems. Daniel wisely navigated the dilemma of obedience without absorption by requesting that his political superior put his proposed diet to the test. He avoided the either-or dilemma of either complete obedience or total separation from society. He remained obedient to political authority while carving out a separateness from his society and political order. He lived for God's kingdom first while remaining obedient to human authority. And in his choice, he would remain dependent on God for his survival or be willing to die to stay faithful.

BENEFITS OF THE DIET DANIEL CHOSE

Quite a few books have been published lately that use "The Daniel Diet" as the basis for healthy living. However, after reading a few, most did not evaluate what Daniel may have eaten. They may have taken their cues from the English translation of the words in the Bible but not from any records of Babylon. That is not to say that such books are worthless; on the contrary, many offer sound advice on healthy eating and living. But Daniel's diet would have looked a little different for him than what the books model for people today.

Babylon produced a variety of meat: sheep, goat, pig, ox, and some chicken. Fish wasn't typical. The average Babylonian rarely ate meat, and the poor could not afford it. They may have had some only at festivals. Babylon, however, was the agricultural breadbasket for the ancient world.

Scholars have determined from cuneiform records and paleobotanical specimens what kinds of foods the Babylonians ate. The primary staple was barley, used for making unleavened bread, and some wheat seasonally harvested. Barley also provided the raw ingredients for their beer, which the upper-class people would have had regularly with their meals. The date palm featured prominently in the Babylonian diet, with over 150 words describing its various parts. A young palm sprout resembled a celery-like vegetable. The Babylonians also harvested pulses, legumes (probably chickpeas, primarily), almonds, and pistachios from local foothills. They would also have had a variety of vegetables such as onion, garlic, leeks, turnips, lettuce, and cucumbers. Linseed and linseed oil would have been harvested locally, and olives and olive oil would have been imported from the coastal area of the Mediterranean. The Babylonian elite likely imported grapes from the coast for their wine as well. Beyond grapes for wine, dates and pomegranates were the most common fruits, as well as apples, figs, pears, and plums. They would have had a variety of spices and aromatic seeds for their dishes, including cress, mustard, cumin, and coriander.[17]

There are several key things to note about this diet. First, the diet would have consisted of *unprocessed* foods, one key to a good diet. Second, this diet would have consisted of what marketing advertisers today call "superfoods." These foods would have been high in protein and carbohydrates and contain appropriate fat. It would have been very high in soluble and insoluble fibers. More importantly, this diet would have been packed with nutrition, including vitamins and minerals, and would have supported good digestive and brain health, which is vital for a young person entering the years in which their brains would be undergoing profound changes.

A third thing to note is that there would be profound health advantages from such a diet. Allium vegetables, including leeks, garlic, and onion, have antibacterial and antiviral properties. Barley is packed with antioxidants, fiber, and vitamins. Almonds are also suitable for brain health and protein. Many of these would have had high concentrations of antioxidants. Combined, this diet would have been conducive to longer life expectancy with far lower expectations of coronary heart disease, cardiovascular disease, certain kinds of cancer, and other chronic diseases.[18]

Based on what we know from the Babylonian scribal records and paleobotanical specimens, Daniel's diet would have been extremely good. His diet would have been very similar to the list of seven species outlined first in Deut 8:8 for the new land overflowing with abundant resources, consisting of "wheat, barley, grapes, figs, pomegranates, olives and date honey." All of these, except olives, were produced in Babylon and were likely familiar to a religious Jew. Olives and olive oil would have been imported. No wonder Daniel served as long as he did in Babylon and the first year of the Persian Empire. He would likely have been in his eighties by then.

Daniel's success with his first appeal will lead to a further, more exotic success with his second. We now turn to that.

---

17. Oates, *Babylon*, 194–95. See also Berry et al., "Middle Eastern," 2290.
18. Berry et al, "Middle Eastern," 2288–95.

5

Daniel's Second Appeal: More Time

By the beginning of Dan 2, we are familiar with Daniel and the setting of his captivity. Daniel 1 provides an overview of the first several years including his forced migration to Babylon, his testing and selection for the rigorous three-year course of study in Babylonian administration, his successful appeal for a restrictive diet, and the subsequent success that he and his three friends experience with their training. Once this training is complete, the king questions their learning and finds none equal to these four young men. But a curious expression toward the end of the chapter warrants our attention. In Dan 1:20, the king finds these four young men "ten times better than all the magicians and enchanters in his whole kingdom." They are not only better than the other students in their cohort but better than all the magicians and enchanters throughout the king's realm. What's going on?

While the division of Daniel's book into chapters makes it look like the story finds a new sequence in chapter 2, upon closer inspection, it appears that the events of the first two chapters overlap. We know from historical records that Nebuchadnezzar defeated the Egyptians at Carchemish sometime in the spring or summer of 605 BC. He returned home quickly, however, because his father, King Nabopolassar, had died. It seems likely that the first year of his reign took place in late 605 to early 604 BC. We don't know precisely when Daniel arrived in Babylon or started his three-year education, but it was likely sometime in 604 BC. Chapter 1 covers the period from 605 to 601 BC, when Daniel and his friends entered service to the Babylonian administration. The text also indicates that Daniel continued to serve Babylon until the first year of King Cyrus, which began with the Persian conquest of Babylon in 539 BC. Daniel would serve in various administrative capacities in two empires for nearly sixty-two years. Thus, in Dan 2, wherein we read of the king's dream and Daniel's involvement with it, begins during Daniel's second year of education and the king's second year of power. Table 4 below illustrates the overlap.

Table 4: Overlap of Daniel 1–2				
605 BC	604 BC	603 BC	602 BC	601 BC
Carchemish	1st regnal year	2nd regnal year	3rd regnal year	4th regnal year
Daniel captive	1st year school	2nd year school King's dream	3rd year school	Begins service

What transpires in Dan 2 reveals there are good reasons why, at the end of Dan 1, Nebuchadnezzar finds Daniel and his friends far better in knowledge and wisdom than the magicians and enchanters of his whole realm at their graduation in 602. In his second regnal year, the king directly observed this young foreign student's wisdom and godly character. He saw Daniel successfully interpret the king's troubling dream and compared this success to the manifest failure of all the other wise men in the face of the king's wrath and commands. Only Daniel had intended to fulfill the king's wishes, whereas the others sought to find a way out of the dilemma posed by the king.

The context for Daniel's second appeal is found in Dan 2:1–13. During the second year of his reign, Nebuchadnezzar had a series of dreams, likely nightmares, that caused him to lose sleep. We don't know how many dreams he had or for how long they persisted, but they troubled the king. Dreams and visions were significant in the religion of Babylonians and could portend major successes or failures. He needed to understand the meaning of his dreams. Because this dream deeply troubled him, he sought out Babylon's professional "wise" men to help him understand it—and likely to provide some relief. We've already noted that the wise men, magicians, enchanters, sorcerers, and astrologers (or Chaldeans) fully subordinated their education and learning to their religious beliefs or at least never separated their professional lives from their religious beliefs. They likely were recruited and trained under Nabopolassar, Nebuchadnezzar's father, and served in his court for a long time, so the king's son would have been familiar with them. These "wise" men may have wanted to "coach" Nebuchadnezzar regarding how administration was done in Babylon.

Daniel in Babylon

Daniel 2:1–3, written in Hebrew, describes Nebuchadnezzar's troubled dreams and his summons to the wise men of Babylon. From Dan 2:4 through the end of Dan 7, the book is written in Aramaic, as these passages are for Jewish and gentile audiences. The astrologers answer the king with the usual formality, "May the king live forever!" and then query the king about the dream's content. Nebuchadnezzar, however, does not reveal the dream to the wise men; instead, he insists that they tell him the content of the dream and the interpretation of it. Did Nebuchadnezzar distrust these wise men of Babylon? Did he doubt their competence to advise him? Or, has he failed to remember the dream, only that it disturbed him? The text does not let on. However, after their initial response, he says that he has firmly decided that they must first tell him the content of the dream before he will believe the interpretation of it or he will have them killed and their homes destroyed. Maybe his dream somehow threatened his rule. They answer again a second time that they need the king to tell them the dream's content before they would interpret it. Nebuchadnezzar becomes convinced that these wise men are stalling for time, perhaps conspiring against him. He tells them there can be only one result should they fail to comply with his request. While the "wise men" group is not a bureaucracy in the modern sense, they tend to behave like one. Though they are composed of disparate people with disparate "skills," they unite to constrain the king's request to something manageable for them. They look out for their lives and shape their responses appropriately.

In their third reply, they inadvertently and unknowingly set the stage for God to intervene dramatically on behalf of Daniel in the unfolding drama. The astrologers answer the king in v. 10, "There is no one on earth who can do what the king asks!" They emphasize their point: "No king, however great and mighty, has ever asked such a thing of any magician or enchanter or astrologer." Whining, they add, "What the king asks is too difficult." Sealing their doom and paving the way to demonstrate God's power through Daniel, they add, "No one can reveal it to the king except the gods, and they do not live among men" (v. 11). So, according to the Babylonian wise men, neither men nor gods can do what the king asks! Just so.

Their response infuriates King Nebuchadnezzar. He is depending on their abilities and threatening them, yet they decline to help. Did Nebuchadnezzar have anger issues? He flies into what may be an irrational rage by ordering the execution of all the wise men of Babylon. His actions foreshadow his rage with Daniel's three friends in Dan 3. Though Daniel and his friends were still in school and not yet part of the professional cadre of Babylonian wise men, they, too, were being searched out for certain death. Then, the text in Dan 2:14–28 and 36 gives us what happens next:

> When Arioch, the commander of the king's guard, had gone out to put to death the wise men of Babylon, Daniel spoke to him with wisdom and tact. He asked the king's officer, "Why did the king issue such a harsh decree?" Arioch then explained the matter to Daniel. At this, Daniel went in to the king and asked for time, so that he might interpret the dream for him.
>
> Then Daniel returned to his house and explained the matter to his friends Hananiah, Mishael and Azariah. He urged them to plead for mercy from the God of heaven concerning this mystery, so that he and his friends might not be executed with the rest of the wise men of Babylon. During the night, the mystery is revealed to Daniel in a vision. Then Daniel praises the God of heaven and says:
> "Praise be to the name of God for ever and ever;
>   wisdom and power are his.
> He changes times and seasons;
>   he deposes kings and raises up others.
> He gives wisdom to the wise
>   and knowledge to the discerning.
> He reveals deep and hidden things;
>   he knows what lies in darkness,
>   and light dwells with him.
> I thank and praise you, God of my ancestors:
>   you have given me wisdom and power,
> you have made known to me what we asked of you,
>   you have made known to us the dream of the king."
>
> Then Daniel went to Arioch, whom the king had appointed to execute the wise men of Babylon, and said to him, "Do not execute the wise men of Babylon. Take me to the king, and I will interpret his dream for him."
>
> Arioch took Daniel to the king at once and said, "I have found a man among the exiles from Judah who can tell the king what his dream means."
>
> The king asked Daniel (also called Belteshazzar), "Are you able to tell me what I saw in my dream and interpret it?"
>
> Daniel replied, "No wise man, enchanter, magician or diviner can explain to the king the mystery he has asked about, but there is a God in heaven who reveals mysteries. He has shown King Nebuchadnezzar what will happen in days to come. Your dream and

the visions that passed through your mind as you lay on your bed are these." . . .

"This was the dream, and now we will interpret it to the king."

Some historical background will help us here. Nabopolassar, possibly an ethnic Chaldean, seized the throne of Babylon in 625 BC and struggled with Assyrian hegemony until 612. It took nearly a decade for Nabopolassar to consolidate his control in Babylon. The Assyrians had ruled Babylon from afar for a very long time and were unwilling to give it up without a fight. But, with the help of the Medes from the western Iranian plateau, which represented a relatively new power in the Mesopotamian area, they defeated Assyria.

At the fall of Assur in 614, Nabopolassar signed a treaty with the Median king, Cyaxeres, and arranged a marriage between his son Nebuchadnezzar and the Median king's granddaughter Amyitis. In 612, a coalition of Babylonians, Medes, and Scythians laid siege to Nineveh, the last redoubt of the Assyrian Empire. After three months, the city fell. The remnant of Assyrians moved to southern Turkey until the Babylonians established a garrison there in 610 BC. The Babylonians continued their campaign (611–609) in the Assyrian hill country until the last Assyrian king fled to Carchemish to await their Egyptian allies, under Pharaoh Necho II, who defeated the small army of Josiah at Megiddo (ca. 608). In around the spring and summer of 605, the crown prince, Nebuchadnezzar, attacked and defeated the remaining Assyrians and the Egyptians at high cost to both sides.[1]

Who are the Medes that Nabopolassar allies with to defeat Assyria, and what role do they play in this part of the story? The Medes were an Iranian people who lived in the north-western portion of modern Iran, slightly east of the Zagros mountains. They were heirs to the Elamite power in southwestern Iran. Very little is known about them, for they kept no records. What little we know about them comes from a few biblical passages but primarily from Assyrian cuneiform writings. Herodotus wrote about them, but historians doubt much of what he says, though not all. Even so, the history of the Medes during the critical period of 650–550 BC remains mostly a mystery. As historian Matt Waters argues, "It remains unclear how we are to move from Assyrian descriptions of the Medes as seemingly independent city-lords to the Medes as a unified force that Cyaxeres (Umakishtar in the Babylonian sources) was able to unleash against Assyria with

---

1. Oates, *Babylon*, 127–28.

such effects in 612 B.C."[2] We get the name Cyaxeres from Herodotus, who wrote his history in the fifth century BC.[3]

Throughout their early history, the Medes were often raided by Assyria to secure essential trade routes and to acquire horses. The Medes were able horsemen. It could be that after so many provocations by Assyria, the independent Medes began uniting against their familiar foe to the west and likely against another possible foe to the east, the Scythians. After defeating Assyria, the Medes left Babylon alone while they ventured north into modern Turkey to conquer Urartu and Lydia. However, Nebuchadnezzar may have had some forebodings about Median ambition late in his reign, as he built a great defensive wall, the Median Wall, which ran from Sippar to Opis to keep out barbarian tribes and to make attack from the north and east more difficult.[4] Certainly, the Medes would play an important role in the eventual destruction of Babylon in 539. Could his dream have portended Median ascendancy over Babylon?

The Medes figured prominently in earlier prophecies. We see Isaiah, who wrote about one hundred years before our story, depict them in Isa 13:17, and Jeremiah, in Jer 25:25–26 and 51:27–27. Jeremiah was a near contemporary of Daniel. In all cases, the prophecies pertain to the eventual destruction of Babylon. While Babylon was not a great power during the early prophecies, it was an essential outpost of the Assyrian Empire. Some critics of the Bible chide the prophets for incorrectly identifying the Medes as the power that will eventually defeat Babylon. But to the Jews at the time, the Medes were the power to behold. The Persians were a minor Iranian people and not a power until the rise of Cyrus (the Great) around 550 BC. But the two become so close that it's impossible to distinguish them by then. Cyrus himself was likely half Mede and half Persian.[5] And the Magi, from Median stock, figured very prominently in Persian affairs of state—culturally, politically, and militarily—more so than any other group apart from the Persians themselves.[6] The Medes played an essential role in the rise of the Persian Empire and the eventual defeat of Babylon toward the end of Daniel's time in political office.

---

2. Waters, *Persia*, 34.
3. Waters, *Persia*, 37.
4. Oates, *Babylon*, 130.
5. Waters, *Persia*, 48–49.
6. Waters, *Persia*, 155.

Ashpenaz, one of the court officials, or eunuchs, also features in this story, though he is never mentioned again in the Bible. Nonetheless, he plays an important role. As already established, Daniel appeals to Ashpenaz not to defile himself with the king's food (vv. 8–10). A little later in the chapter, Ashpenaz appoints an anonymous guard (v. 11) over Daniel and his three friends. We never get to learn his name. But he must have communicated with Ashpenaz in some fashion, for, after making his appeal to Ashpenaz, Daniel asks this anonymous guard to test the quality of the proposed alternative diet. We never learn whether the guard or Ashpenaz judged the quality of Daniel's alternative diet, though the text implies it was the guard himself.

In Dan 2, we meet a new official positioned hierarchically somewhere between Ashpenaz and this anonymous guard. He is Arioch, the commander of the guards. Not much is told about him in the text, but it seems likely that Daniel may have developed a good reputation with both the guard and Ashpenaz. If so, that reputation would have spread to Arioch, who plays a vital role in Daniel's second appeal. During the crisis of the king's epic anger outburst and the subsequent efforts to manage it, Arioch gives considerable latitude to Daniel to appeal for more time and clemency.

THE APPEAL

Again, several things stand out about this appeal as well. As in his earlier appeal, Daniel demonstrates wisdom and patience beyond his years. He never steps outside of the boundaries of political authority. Because of his first appeal in Dan 1, he likely developed an excellent reputation with the people he worked with. But he moves and speaks with humility and respect, intending to solve the king's problem. Wisdom seeks solutions for problems that have no clear-cut answers.

Daniel and his friends continued the excellent and diligent work they had begun in Dan 1:20. Because they subordinated themselves to the political authority of Babylon, they continued to hold great promise for the king's service. And because Daniel successfully appealed to a very senior member of the Babylonian administration, when Arioch looks to gather and execute the "wise" men of Babylon, he pauses long enough to give Daniel a chance to ask his question. Given that opening, Daniel tactfully and wisely asks why the decree was so harsh or urgent. Arioch explains the decree and seemingly permits Daniel to ask the king for some time. The

DANIEL'S SECOND APPEAL: MORE TIME

only thing that may explain Arioch's confidence in (1) granting Daniel an answer to his questions and (2) permitting him to ask the king for time is that Daniel's reputation for wisdom, tact, humility, and success was how God continued to grant him "favor and compassion" in the sight of the governing authorities.

Daniel does something else to prepare for his second appeal. He seeks out all the facts of the situation. Instead of listening to the gossip around the "water cooler" about the king's decision to execute all the wise men, Daniel sought out Arioch, the person tasked with implementing the king's order. He ignores second or third-hand information on which to base his decision, though most of us would likely want to find any way to escape in a panic. But better decisions can only come with better information. Because of his request and likely his reputation, Arioch explains the situation to Daniel.

We will also see that Daniel and his three friends continue to prepare by being a consistent and persistent community of like-minded believers. What can be inferred from Daniel's discussion and appeal in Dan 1 is seen more clearly in Dan 2:17-18: Daniel and his friends are a praying community of believers. After explaining the situation to his three friends, he requests them to pray specifically for an answer to the king's problem, not for the king to change his mind or for God to soften his heart. He understands that the king has a real problem, or at least what he perceives as a real problem. He urges them to plead for God's mercy for an answer so that they will not be executed along with the other wise men of Babylon.

To advance politically and bureaucratically, lower members of a political apparatus will frequently align themselves with the careers of senior people for protection and opportunities. Mentors are expected to help mentees advance in their careers with the reciprocal expectation that junior partners will support the aspirations of their mentors. Although they are in the king's service, Daniel and his friends don't seek out a patron to protect them. Perhaps because they were Jewish, they had no option to seek out the protection of a patron within the Babylonian administration. Still, Daniel nonetheless made "friends" through the success of his early appeal. However, nothing in the text indicates that he relies on anyone other than God for advancement and protection.

Notice that in his appeal, Daniel never challenges the authority or right of the king to execute the wise men of Babylon. In his tactful questioning of Arioch, the guards' commander, Daniel merely asks to understand the harshness of the king's order. Daniel lived with the knowledge that political authority given to kings and governments includes the delegated authority to use lethal force, whether against internal or external enemies. This does not mean every decision to use force is thereby right in God's eyes or ours. Daniel, however, never debates whether Nebuchadnezzar's decision was just or not. Was it because he believed the king was just? Did he realize he could not challenge the king's authority? Or do we see Daniel behaving wisely under the sovereign constraints of his conditions? Given all we see of Daniel throughout the book, I believe Daniel models wise living under extreme conditions.

As part of his appeal, Daniel then goes to see the king and asks for a little more time so that he might interpret the dream for him. Did he actually speak with the king? Does Arioch permit him to see the king? By all accounts, Daniel doesn't enlist the help of Ashpenaz, the chief of the court officials, who helped Daniel with his first appeal. But Arioch must have known Daniel's reputation through Ashpenaz and perhaps his guard. So, either Daniel went in on his own to see the king or Arioch must have somehow had confidence in Daniel to allow him to seek a little more time from the king, perhaps hoping (trusting) that Daniel could do what the professional wise men of Babylon were incapable of doing. Daniel was likely granted little time, maybe only twenty-four hours, to solve the king's problem. As in the first appeal, Daniel sought to accomplish the intended goal of the king: an interpretation of the dream. The king, or Arioch on behalf of the king, would likely have seen Daniel's new appeal as credible because of his reputation.

Daniel makes several appeals in Dan 2. In addition to appealing to the king, Daniel appeals to his friends to pray for mercy from the God of heaven, which they join him in doing. His friends could have said no. Along with them, he appeals to God to answer the king's concerns about the dream's content and interpretation. God could have declined, as well. Daniel appeals to Arioch not to execute the wise men on behalf of the king, which Arioch could have declined. Daniel finally seeks to present the results of God's answer to the king's concerns by requesting to have an audience to share his understanding of the dream. Given how poorly the professional wise men behaved, Nebuchadnezzar could have also declined. Was he still enraged? At the very least, the king was deeply unsettled. We don't know for sure. But there was something disarming about Daniel's approach, his appeal.

What makes an appeal so appealing? An appeal signifies a request where one side demonstrates dependence upon the other for help. It comes from a position of vulnerability and is the best way for the weaker to ask something of the stronger. Demanding, protesting, or throwing fits seem less likely to elicit cooperation. A righteous appeal done righteously with humility threatens no one and demonstrates God's kingdom power, a power based on our weakness and his greatness.

Daniel also gave credit where credit was due—to God. When he understands the mystery provided by God in a vision during the night, Daniel praises the God of heaven personally with his soulful soliloquy (vv. 20–23), one of the most explicit statements of God's sovereign rule over the kingdom of men in the Bible. While Daniel likely had some inkling of God's sovereign rule, at least from reading Scriptures consistently, this epic revelation must have increased his understanding of God's sovereignty with greater clarity than ever before. He not only understood God's sovereign constraints on his life but now fully grasped God's sovereign constraints on political leaders in history and into the future. How much confidence would that have given him to pursue righteous political living?

He also uses the occasion to praise God before the king without pushiness or self-righteousness. In perfect timing, the king asks Daniel, "Are you able to tell me what I saw in my dream and interpret it?" (v. 26). The wise men had only recently said, "There is no one on earth who can do what the kings asks!" (v. 10). They further added that "no one can reveal it to the king except the gods, and they do not live among men" (v. 11). Daniel agrees with the sentiment of the wise men by saying, "No wise man, enchanter, magician or diviner can explain to the king the mystery he has asked about, but there is a God in heaven who reveals mysteries" (vv. 27–28). He takes the focus off of himself, off the "wise" men, off the false gods of Babylon, and puts the focus and praise squarely on the God of heaven. The wise men correctly answered the king because they did not have a relationship with the living God of heaven and history. Daniel makes it explicit now.

Daniel goes further and spreads the blessings of God's deliverance. After hearing from Arioch about the king's decree, Daniel calls his friends to request that they pray to escape execution along with the wise men of Babylon. The text indicates nothing other than a petition to God to answer the king's problem. Nowhere in the text do we see Daniel critiquing or criticizing the religion of the wise men. Nowhere does Daniel disparage the corruption that was likely endemic in this priestly caste's ranks, behavior, and practices. He was undoubtedly aware of it from what he recorded Nebuchadnezzar saying about them. However, after God reveals the mystery to Daniel, Nebuchadnezzar stays Arioch's hand from executing the wise men. Was he giving the wise men an opportunity to come to understand who the God of heaven truly is?

Daniel continues to respect and never challenge the political authority of the king. He appropriately uses the "chain of command" by going to the correct person, Arioch. He doesn't try to jump over the commander charged with carrying out the king's command, by, say, going to Ashpenaz or someone else. Further, in this appeal, he only asks Arioch why the king's decree was so harsh. The Aramaic word for harsh here can mean either "harsh" or "urgent," a term that other translations use instead of harsh.[7] Urgency certainly seems more appropriate to the context of the text, as the king commissioned Arioch to collect all the wise men of Babylon for execution. It's not hard to imagine Arioch having to catch his breath to hear Daniel's question. Arioch or the king likely only gave Daniel a very short time to petition God to solve this mystery.

Daniel also avoids using any influence he may have had. Recall that Daniel appealed to Ashpenaz in Dan 1. He didn't try to use his relationship with Ashpenaz to avoid the fate of the wise men. Nor does it appear he used any influence or patrons to help him with the problem he faced. No, the only one Daniel relied on was the God of heaven. Throughout his second appeal, he continually sought permission by appealing to others to find out the reasons for the king's decree, to get time from the king to pray for a resolution to the mystery, to get his friends to join him in prayer to God, to seek God's wisdom on what the king dreamed and how to interpret it, and to approach the king with the resolution of the mystery.

After God reveals the mystery to Daniel, more wonderful things happen. Daniel approaches Arioch and asks that he stay the execution of the wise men and allow him to present the king with God's answer. Arioch then takes Daniel to the king but tells him that he (Arioch) found someone among the Jewish exiles who can explain the dream. Daniel never contradicts Arioch and instead allows him to take the credit. It may sound small, but this is another hallmark of Daniel's humility. He does not boast or take credit because the solution to the king's nightmares is God's doing, not his. Further, he never lords it over the wise men that he solved the problem of the king's dreams when they couldn't. There's no trace anywhere or at any time of self-righteousness or self-aggrandizement from Daniel.

---

7. *ESV Study Bible*, 1588.

DANIEL'S SECOND APPEAL: MORE TIME

As a young person, Daniel remains remarkably calm in the face of near-certain death by the king's decree. Young people, in particular, are neurologically more likely to "flip their lids" when confronted with challenging, demanding, or extreme situations. Psychiatrists and neuroscientists point out that the brain's limbic system is hardwired to detect threats to the body and will respond to threats of annihilation milliseconds faster than the executive function of the brain, the prefrontal cortex.[8] When we "flip our lid," our survival mechanism reacts faster but makes more inaccurate assumptions and inferences about the situation. Between ages 14 and 24 or so, young people undergo rapid pruning and replacing of neurons in the brain to prepare for adult life. They tend to feel issues of justice, of right and wrong, far more strongly than earlier or later in life. Because of this, their limbic system fires red hot very often, as anyone with teenagers in their household will know. When the limbic system fires off, the prefrontal cortex (the executive function) can go offline for some time, resulting in anger, defensiveness, and feelings of injustice and wrongness, which can overpower longer-term reasoning.

Yet Daniel not only displays calmness in the face of threats to his life and that of his friends but also engages the executive functioning part of his brain. He expertly phrases his appeals to ensure the maximum possibility of success. Notice how, in v. 15, Daniel seeks out the facts of the matter while maintaining respect for authority and never questions the right of political authority to carry out the king's decree. He seeks out information before he makes his decision to appeal for time. He relies on facts, not limbic-system-generated interpretations of the situation, and he doesn't rely on second and third-hand information.

Daniel seeks a little time to make the interpretation known when he appeals. This would have been tricky for him, given that Nebuchadnezzar believed the wise men were playing for time. But he makes it clear that the time he needs is not open ended, nor is he engaging in delaying tactics. He seeks to make the interpretation known. He strives to fulfill both the intention and the desire of the king. How refreshing would his appeal have been to the king who had only recently "flipped his lid" over the stonewalling of the wise men? The king now has someone who seeks to meet his desire.

Daniel never stepped outside the bounds of his servant relationship to political authority. Even when he tells Arioch to stay the execution of the wise men, he later lets Arioch take credit for finding someone who could

---

8. See Siegel, *Brainstorm*, 101–10.

help the king. Nor does he challenge political authority and rail against the "injustice" of the king's urgent and harsh decree. He merely responds to the urgency of the order. He never gets self-righteous about his appeal nor about his "success" in appealing to God through prayer for an answer to Nebuchadnezzar's mysterious dreams.

Daniel gives credit where credit is due: to the God of heaven. He praises God, who solved the dilemma for Daniel and answered his request for the content of the dream and its interpretation. Daniel also credits King Nebuchadnezzar. In v. 28, Daniel tells the king that God "has shown King Nebuchadnezzar what will happen in days to come." According to Daniel, God honored Nebuchadnezzar with the dream, and the king should be grateful to the God of Heaven for having them (without telling him to be thankful!). He praises the king for being a worthy vessel of such vital information.

Nebuchadnezzar honors Daniel at the end of chapter 2. He orders that an offering and incense be given to Daniel and acknowledges that Daniel serves a mighty God. He says, "Surely your God is the God of gods and the LORD of kings and a revealer of mysteries, for you were able to reveal this mystery" (v. 47). Then, at some point later, he promotes Daniel to administer the province of Babylon and puts him in charge of all the wise men. We're not given a time-stamp at the end of this chapter that indicates when this occurs, except that it is after the initial offering and incense. Since Daniel was still in his second year of schooling, and we know from the end of chapter 1 that the king evaluates Daniel and his Jewish colleagues as outstanding graduates, he must have been put into such a leadership position upon his graduation, sometime around 601 BC. Still, he would have been very young, around nineteen years old. Daniel also spreads the blessings further and requests that his three friends be given significant political appointments. The king agrees. It seems likely that, while the king intended to honor Daniel, these promotions may have set in motion the jealousy of the other wise men that led to the attempt to entrap Daniel's friends in Dan 3. Though Daniel would likely be "untouchable" because of his close connection with the king, his three friends would be more vulnerable to the bureaucratic machinations of the other "wise" men of Babylon.

THE DREAM AND ITS INTERPRETATION

Critics of the book of Daniel usually do not care for chapters 7–12 as they are apocalyptic and reveal what is to come. They tend to dismiss these chapters

DANIEL'S SECOND APPEAL: MORE TIME

as written later after the events, somewhere during the second century BC. Of course, that doesn't solve all their problems with the book of Daniel. This is partly because Nebuchadnezzar's dream of the statue in chapter 2 is also apocalyptic. It reveals different kingdoms, from the present time of the dream and on into history to include something like our day or the end of days. There will be a final kingdom, one not made by human beings but a rock that smashes the last kingdom, the kingdom of iron and clay. This has been understood to be the inauguration of God's kingdom on earth, which started when Jesus announced the kingdom was at hand and would be finalized at a later time.

Daniel reveals that the image in Nebuchadnezzar's dream was a giant statue of a man. On top was a head of gold. Below the head was a chest and arms of silver. The belly and thighs of the statute were of bronze. Its legs were of iron, and its feet were partly iron and clay. These metals were well known to the ancients of this time, as they are to us today, but the clay may have been something like the clay the Babylonians fired in furnaces to make bricks for their impressive building campaign. The furnace in Dan 3 that Daniel's three friends will be forced to endure may have been used to fire clay bricks.

Daniel interprets the dream. The head of gold was Nebuchadnezzar's political reign. Daniel mentions what makes the head of gold—that is, Nebuchadnezzar's reign—superior to the subsequent kingdoms. In vv. 37–38, Daniel says, "Your majesty, you are the king of kings. The God of heaven has given you dominion and power and might and glory; in your hands he has placed all mankind and the beasts of the field and the birds of the sky. Wherever they live, he has made you ruler over them all. You are that head of gold."

The silver of the chest and arms represents a new political order that will be "inferior to yours" (v. 39). The silver represents the Medo-Persian Empire that began under the reign of Cyrus the Great. A third kingdom, understood to be the Macedonian (sometimes called Greek) Empire and its successors, are represented by bronze and "will rule over the whole earth." Finally, a fourth kingdom, the Roman Empire, is represented by iron and will rule by force. The feet of clay mixed with iron are understood to be some future kingdoms that arise from the Roman Empire, or, likely, future gentile kingdoms, which rule until the time God's kingdom establishes itself on earth.

Table 5 below illustrates how the four empires are treated throughout the book of Daniel.

Table 5: Dreams and Visions of Empires in Daniel				
Empire	Ch. 2 dream	Ch. 7 vision	Ch. 8 vision	Years
Babylonian	Head of God	Lion		626–539 BC
Medo-Persian	Chest of silver	Bear	Ram	550–330 BC
Greek (and Ptolemies and Seleucids)	Belly of bronze	Leopard	Goat	330–63 BC
Roman	Legs of iron	Frightening beast		63 BC–AD 120

Daniel's interpretation may be puzzling in some ways. In what sense was Babylon superior to subsequent gentile kingdoms? As we will see below, the land area under the sovereign control of the various empires depicted in Nebuchadnezzar's dream starts to expand slowly (with Babylon), expands greatly under Cyrus, shrinks somewhat under Alexander the Great, and never achieves the same extent under Rome. The size of these empires are listed below in table 6.

Table 6: Size of Four Empires of Daniel[9]			
Empire	*Mmi^2	Percent world population	Peak size/year
Babylonian	.19	.19 percent	562 BC
Medo-Persian	2.12	4.08 percent	500 BC
Macedonian/Greek	2.01	3.86 percent	323 BC
Roman	1.93	3.71 percent	AD 117
*Mmi^2 = million square miles			

Political scientist Rein Taagapera provides some objective measures of the power of various empires. He does so by measuring the land area of different empires throughout history. Taagapera argues that "'Empire' designates any relatively large sovereign political entity whose components are not sovereign."[10] He also suggests that "empire size at any given time is defined as the dry land area it controls, at least in the sense of having some undisputed military and taxation prerogatives."[11] He acknowledges that empire size *may* not relate to an empire's cultural, spiritual, or commercial

9. Table 6 is based on Taagepera, "3000 to 600 B.C.," 186–87; and Taagepera, "600 B.C. to 600 A.D.," 115–18.

10. Taagepera, "600 B.C. 600 A.D.," 117.

11. Taagepera, "600 B.C. to 600 A.D.," 119.

power. Carthage, for example, was a commercial empire that rivaled Rome for a time, though it was many times smaller in land area. However, Rome eventually defeated it. Since we do not have good records of the actual wealth and influence of historical empires, their so-called soft power, and population size has only limited and indirect support for state power, land area is the one thing that can be unambiguously measured. We have much better records of hard power, activities such as military conquests and occupations of former enemies' political terrain.

Babylon is by far the smallest of the four empires listed. As the first in history to jump above more than two million square miles in land area, the Persian Empire is the largest. Cyrus may have supersized his empire by innovating satrapies (provinces) and delegating limited power to local provinces. Alexander the Great only conquered about 90 percent of the land area of the Persian Empire. "Alexander was not an empire-founder but an empire-seizer who arrested the decline of the Iranian empire for a few years."[12] Separately, Rome carved out its own smaller empire, and in the east, it did so at the expense of the leftover Greek empires. On a map, it is apparent that these four empires' geographical expansion was horizontal, which is typical for empires throughout history. Something like 80 percent of all historical empires before the age of steamships and newer technology expanded in this way, as they found it much easier to project military and political power within the same ecological zone.[13]

The peak size of the empires suggests something interesting as well. Babylon's peak year of size was 562 BC, at the death of Nebuchadnezzar. Several more kings ruled until Persia conquered Babylon in 539 BC, but none had the vigor of the second king. The peak size for Persia, however, was in 500 BC, about thirty years after the death of Cyrus, during the reign of his greatest successor, Darius. The peak size of the Greek/Macedonian Empire was in 323 BC, at the death of Alexander. His heirs divided the kingdom into four areas, two of which subsequently dominated the post-Macedonian world in the West (Ptolemaic and Seleucid). The peak size for Rome was in AD 117, nearly fifty years after the destruction of the temple in Jerusalem and many years after the founding of the Roman Empire. This, along with something Daniel suggests in Dan 2:36, indicates that the greatness of these human kingdoms had to do with the coherence and effectiveness of the political rule during these times. That is to say, it has

---

12. Taagepera, "600 B.C. to 600 A.D.," 123.
13. Turchin et al., "East-West," 226.

to do with how powerfully these rulers ruled during their reigns. Nebuchadnezzar ruled over his kingdom with almost absolute efficiency and authority. Cyrus and subsequent kings ruled their empire less efficiently. Nebuchadnezzar was able to enact and modify Babylonian laws with complete sovereignty (Dan 2:12, 48), whereas Darius (under Persian rule) was powerless to change the "laws of the Medes and the Persians" (Dan 6:8–9; Esth 1:9, 8:8). Alexander the Great's real genius was in military conquest, not in ruling. Neither did he live very long once he conquered his empire. While still an empire, Rome had to contend with more and more checks on the emperors' power. Over time, the relative power of all rulers depicted in this dream diminishes until other human kingdoms conquer it.

Note that the statue in Nebuchadnezzar's dream also ignores other powerful states and empires throughout history. During the peak years of Roman rule (AD 117), when Rome had a land area of some 1.93 million square miles, Han China had over 2.5 million square miles. Subsequently, other empires have come to occupy much greater land areas, including China, Russia, Canada, Brazil, and Australia. Taagapera says, "During the last 800 years, three empires (Mongol, British, Russian) reached more than 8 million square miles."[14] The central focus of the statue, however, is on empires that control the destiny of the faithful remnant of Jews and later believers. To that end, the dream would ignore other empires.

The key, of course, to this apocalyptic dream may be found only by looking at all of the visions throughout Daniel. It's not just the greatness of human, gentile kingdoms that is at issue. It is also a fact that righteous people throughout history can expect trouble from these gentile rulers. Gentile kingdoms, however regarded by human standards of power and greatness, pursue the rulers' interests, not God's. They never pursue God's interests except incidentally, when God directs their hearts, as we have seen before. And, as Rev 13 and 17 make clear, these rulers will join together to fight the Lord himself and his followers.

But Daniel interprets the dream to mean so much more than the greatness of human kingdoms. Of course, their "greatness" is more about brutal control in the selfish pursuit of power. But all human kingdoms come to an end, usually at the hands of other kingdoms and through different forms of internal decay (environmental, spiritual, or cultural, as well as diminished resources). And the final kingdom or kingdoms of man will end at the hand of God. The final kingdom(s) in Nebuchadnezzar's dream will be marked by

---

14. Taagepera, "600 B.C. to A.D. 600," 109.

both strength (iron) and weakness (clay), indicating that such kingdoms will have a hard time maintaining their rule. Daniel interprets the dream: "As the toes were partly iron and partly clay, so this kingdom will be partly strong and partly brittle. And just as you saw the iron mixed with baked clay, so the people will be a mixture and will not remain united, any more than iron mixes with clay" (vv. 42–43). The authority and reason for the state's power at this time will be far more brittle than it was during the reign of Nebuchadnezzar and even of the subsequent kingdoms in Nebuchadnezzar's dream.

Daniel's interpretation of the apocalyptic dream seems to suggest that it will become more complex and more challenging for gentile political regimes to hold on to their legitimacy and authority even while appearing to be ruthlessly strong toward their citizens. We see something like this from time to time today. The Soviet Union, which looked powerful in the 1970s and 1980s, crumbled quickly once the political leadership lost its legitimacy with those it ruled. Like dominoes, a whole rash of subordinate and allied nations under Soviet sway followed when Soviet legitimacy was called into question. China has elements of both the harshness of political power and the fragility of legitimacy. Its harshness and weakness were on full display during the Tiananmen crisis in 1989 and continue today even as it colonizes Hong Kong and threatens Taiwan and the islands in the South China Sea. Both empires have been noted for their persecution of believers.

Daniel was born in Jerusalem only to be taken hostage by a foreign, authoritarian power. In chapter 2, we read he was tested and was found to remain politically subordinate to the governing authorities. He remained humble yet supportive of those in power and used his wisdom to make his appeals to his friends, political authorities, and, most importantly, to God. He found a way to flourish in an otherwise hostile political system by remaining committed to God's kingdom purposes that may not have been fully obvious to him in his early days. However, through his second appeal, Daniel received through the dreams of Nebuchadnezzar a "God's eye view" of the unfolding historical drama of the nations and the future of his people. What role will he continue to play? Let's turn to the next chapter to learn.

6

Daniel's Third Appeal: A Non-Appeal with Appeal

THE BOOK OF DANIEL begins early in the reign of Nebuchadnezzar with Daniel's first and second appeals, likely during the king's first two years in power (604–3 BC). We now move to much later in Daniel's administrative career in Babylon (539 BC), after he interprets the handwriting on the wall (Dan 5) that reveals God's judgment to King Belshazzar that the Medes and the Persians will conquer Babylon. We encounter Daniel making another appeal just after the Babylonian conquest, during the first year of Darius the Mede. Though later in the book of Daniel, chapters 7 and 8 will relate visions Daniel had earlier during Belshazzar's term as co-regent with his father, Nabonidus (553 and 551 BC). But we have little information beyond Daniel's early years with Nebuchadnezzar and his dreams and visions during the reign of Belshazzar, and we have virtually no records of what Nebuchadnezzar did for most of his forty-two-year reign other than his early military conquests and building campaign. There are significant gaps in the narrative of the Babylonian Empire, though we know it had five or six kings, depending on how you judge Belshazzar's rule as co-regent.

DANIEL'S THIRD APPEAL: A NON-APPEAL WITH APPEAL

The kings of Babylon are depicted in table 7:

Table 7: Kings of Babylon			
King	Dates	Relationship	Daniel mentioned
Nabopolassar	626–605 BC	Founder	
Nebuchadnezzar	605–562 BC	Son of Nabopolassar	Early
Evil-Marodach	562–560 BC	Son of Nebuchadnezzar	
Neriglissar	560–556 BC	Son-in-law of Nebuchadnezzar	
Nabonidus	556–539 BC	Usurper	
Belshazzar	553–539 BC	Son of Nabonidus	Early to late

If Daniel had been about fifteen years of age when he was taken captive (605 BC), he would have been around eighty during the first year of Darius's reign. The vegetarian diet he and his friends opted for while in their three-year training program in Babylonian administration served him well physically and cognitively.

While we don't know what Daniel was doing during the intervening years, there are some intriguing clues about his activities. In Dan 4, Nebuchadnezzar has another dream that requires interpretation. He brought all his wise men in to interpret the dream, and unlike before, he told them the content of the dream. Again, the wise men fail to discern its meaning. Finally, chapter 4 records that the king brought Daniel in and mentions him by his given name as chief of the wise men. Daniel interprets the dream and, for the first time, prophetically encourages the king to repent. Of course, the king doesn't, and a year later, the judgment is passed, and the king suffers seven times before he acknowledges the glory of the God of heaven. Was this early in the king's reign? We don't know because the text doesn't say. But Daniel is chief of the wise men by this point. Moreover, the king asks first for his wise men, and only when they fail does Daniel come to help interpret the dream. Since Nebuchadnezzar is reigning, this must occur in 600 BC or later.

After Nebuchadnezzar's reign, does Daniel get demoted, sidelined, or removed from his role as chief of the wise men? If so, his demotion might have been during the reign of Nabonidus, sometime around 556 BC. All the Chaldean kings of Babylon, from Nebuchadnezzar through Neriglissar, paid homage to the god of Babylon, Marduk. Nabonidus, however, was of Assyrian heritage and worshipped the moon god, Sin, not the traditional god of Babylon.[1] Our clue for Daniel's possible demotion may be found in Dan 5. When Belshazzar, Nabonidus' son, is confounded by the handwriting on the wall, he calls in the wise men to do for him what they couldn't do for Nebuchadnezzar. In Dan 5:8, it says that all the wise men came in. Daniel had been appointed chief of the wise men during Nebuchadnezzar's time, but where was he now? In v. 11, his mother, the queen, has to tell Belshazzar, "There is a man in your kingdom who has the spirit of the holy gods in him. In the time of your father [i.e., referring to the great king, Nebuchadnezzar, a tradition of the ancient world][2] he was found to have insight and intelligence and wisdom like that of the gods." Interestingly, no one else mentions Daniel except for the queen's mother. Belshazzar wasn't familiar with Daniel or his reputation, or at least forgot about him.

The next clue is in Dan 8, during the third year of Belshazzar's reign (551 BC). Daniel has his second vision in this chapter, and it expands upon his first (Dan 7). The key clue here is that Daniel sees himself in the citadel of Susa in the province of Elam near the Ulai Canal. Susa is the southeasternmost part of the Mesopotamian floodplain. It was also the headquarters for the ancient Elamite Empire, which both Media and Persia claimed as ancestral.[3] Daniel likely had traveled to Susa in his administrative duties to recognize what he was seeing. Or, perhaps, he had been posted there later in his career or even retired to the region.

He was placed in various positions of governance for a very long time. As such, Daniel would have become intimately familiar not only with the internal administration of the Babylonian Empire but also with its foreign relations with other regional powers in the area. Especially if he spent any time in Susa, he would likely have heard a great deal about the Medes and, subsequently, the Persians. Recall that the Medes played a vital role as an ally to Nebuchadnezzar's father, Nabopolassar, in finally defeating the Assyrian Empire in the seventh century, when Daniel was born. The Medes remained a great power until sometime in 550 BC when Cyrus overthrew King Astyages of Media and united the Medes and Persians into a new empire. He would have been well acquainted with their fierce military

---

1. Kriwaczek, *Babylon*, 274.

2. The ancients usually referred to the most well-known of their predecessors as their father. See Archer, *Survey*, 391.

3. Durant, *Oriental Heritage*, 117; Waters, *Ancient Persia*, 9, 21–22, 34. See also Wikipedia, "Susa."

reputation as he interpreted the "handwriting on the wall" during the final day of Belshazzar's rule.

The Medo-Persian Empire conquered Babylon in 539 BC without a fight. While much has been written about the Persian Empire's general characteristics, we don't know many things. The Medes themselves never kept records of their empire. What we see of them primarily comes from Assyrian cuneiform writings. The Persians also left no official history of their empire. Historian Matt Waters writes, "The ancient Persians themselves wrote almost nothing—at least nothing that has survived—in the form of narrative history. As with many ancient peoples, records of the past were kept alive through oral tradition."[4] Much of what we know about Persia and its kings comes from later Greek historians, particularly Herodotus, writing in the middle of the fifth century or later. Herodotus collects the various oral traditions and gives the reader his best interpretation. The problem, as Waters notes, is that a significant amount of attention has to be paid to "the problems of historical analysis engendered by the paucity of sources as well as the tendentiousness of those that are available."[5] The tendentiousness Waters refers to is this: Greek historians wrote to Greek audiences with Greek cultural biases, not necessarily writing in a way that modern historians would or should (i.e., objectively). His history may have been written for a public audience—say, in the theaters of Greece—and so he would likely have written things with the Greek understanding of tragedy and the Greek fascination and repulsion for Persian culture.

Who is Darius the Mede? This becomes a problem when interpreting a part of the text in Dan 6. The previous chapter ends with, "Darius the Mede took over the kingdom, at the age of sixty-two." Later, chapter 9 begins with, "In the first year of Darius son of Xerxes (a Mede by descent), who was made ruler over the Babylonian kingdom—in the first year of his reign..."

Historically, we know that Cyrus had conquered the Medes in 550 BC. He led the combined kingdom of Medes and Persians in the conquest of Babylon in 539 BC. But we have yet to find an official record of anyone named Darius being made king of Babylon. The only Darius is a later king of Persia, Cyrus's greatest successor, who was in power about twenty years afterward. Is the book of Daniel in error here? Some critics point to this as a historical error by Daniel. Other commentators and theologians have

---

4. Waters, *Persia*, 11.
5. Waters, *Persia*, 8.

tested various ideas to answer this question, but none of them are thoroughly satisfying. Was this Darius a Median general named Gubaru, identified in Babylonian inscriptions as being installed as governor? If so, why does Daniel call him Darius? Or (more likely) does Daniel refer to Cyrus with his Babylonian throne name of Darius the Mede? We have some clues.

Herodotus records his favored oral tradition: Cyrus was half Mede and half Persian. In the story he accepts, after rejecting more outlandish ones, the Median king Astyages has a dream of his daughter Mandane giving birth to the eventual ruler of the Medes, so he gives her in marriage to a lesser Persian noble, Cambyses. He thinks this will solve the problem as the Persians were considered a minor ethnicity. Astyages subsequently dreams something even more disturbing, however: a prophecy of conquest by the offspring of Mandane. Astyages decides to have her child killed. However, the child (Cyrus) is protected by an outsider and eventually fulfills the king's vision and dream and usurps the throne. Cyrus, half Persian, half Mede, was likely born in 600 BC, so that would have made him about sixty-one or sixty-two by the time of the Babylonian conquest. That fits with the age of this Darius.

At the end of Dan 6, the text mentions Darius and Cyrus, the Persian, together in the same sentence. Are these two separate people, or is something else going on? While we may never confidently know, biblical scholar D. J. Wiseman has suggested a likely solution. Wiseman first proposed in 1957 and updated in 1965[6] that we should look to the book of Daniel for evidence for who this earlier Darius was, and he finds a startling piece in Dan 6:28, where it says, "So Daniel prospered during the reign of Darius and the reign of Cyrus the Persian." He proposes, with some good linguistic and circumstantial evidence, that Cyrus had more than one name. We know from history that he had many different names based on the places he conquered: King of Anshan (his homeland and referencing Elam ancestors who were kings of Anshan and Susa), King of the World, Great King, Strong King, King of Babylon, King of Sumer and Akkad, and King of the Four Quarters.[7]

Wiseman suggests Cyrus was known as Darius the Mede to the Babylonians and Medes. To the Persians and subsequent history, he was known as Cyrus the Persian (or Cyrus the Great) because of Persia's subsequent

---

6. For his later analysis and further development, see Wiseman, "Historical Problems," 12–14.

7. Waters, *Persia*, 49–50.

ascendancy over the Median tribes and incorporation of them into Persian identity. Wiseman points out the Hebrew appositional use of "and" suggests it could be translated as "Darius, that is to say (or, even), Cyrus the Persian."[8] It was used in this way in Scripture for an Assyrian king. In 1 Chr 5:26, the text says, "So the God of Israel stirred up the spirit of Pul king of Assyria (that is, Tiglath-Pileser king of Assyria)." The same Hebrew appositional is used here in this passage as well.

I am taking Daniel's side in this debate. Given that he was an insider in the Babylonian and subsequent Persian administrations, he likely knew some things we would never be privy to. Daniel regards Darius as King, perhaps Cyrus's Babylonian court name, and it seems wise to follow his lead as we analyze his subsequent appeal. The most likely hypothesis is that Darius the Mede is how the Babylonians referred to Cyrus the Persian. It's only later, historically, that Cyrus became regarded as Cyrus the Great.

THE APPEAL

Dan 6:1–16:

> It pleased Darius to appoint 120 satraps to rule throughout the kingdom, with three administrators over them, one of whom was Daniel. The satraps were made accountable to them so that the king might not suffer loss. Now Daniel so distinguished himself among the administrators and the satraps by his exceptional qualities that the king planned to set him over the whole kingdom. At this, the administrators and the satraps tried to find grounds for charges against Daniel in his conduct of government affairs, but they were unable to do so. They could find no corruption in him, because he was trustworthy and neither corrupt nor negligent. Finally these men said, "We will never find any basis for charges against this man Daniel unless it has something to do with the law of his God."
>
> So the administrators and the satraps went as a group to the king and said: "May King Darius live forever! The royal administrators, prefects, satraps, advisers and governors have all agreed that the king should issue an edict and enforce the decree that anyone who prays to any god or man during the next thirty days, except to you, Your Majesty, shall be thrown into the lions' den. Now, Your Majesty, issue the decree and put it in writing so that it

---

8. Wiseman, "Historical Problems," 12–13.

cannot be altered—in accordance with the laws of the Medes and the Persians, which cannot be repealed." So King Darius put the decree in writing.

Now when Daniel learned that the decree had been published, he went home to his upstairs room where the windows opened toward Jerusalem. Three times a day he got down on his knees and prayed, giving thanks to his God, just as he had done before. Then these men went as a group and found Daniel praying and asking God for help. So they went to the king and spoke to him about his royal decree: "Did you not publish a decree that during the next thirty days anyone who prays to any god or man except to you, Your Majesty, would be thrown into the lions' den?"

The king answered, "The decree stands—in accordance with the laws of the Medes and the Persians, which cannot be repealed."

Then they said to the king, "Daniel, who is one of the exiles from Judah, pays no attention to you, Your Majesty, or to the decree you put in writing. He still prays three times a day." When the king heard this, he was greatly distressed; he was determined to rescue Daniel and made every effort until sundown to save him.

Then the men went as a group to King Darius and said to him, "Remember, Your Majesty, that according to the law of the Medes and the Persians no decree or edict that the king issues can be changed."

So the king gave the order, and they brought Daniel and threw him into the lions' den. The king said to Daniel, "May your God, whom you serve continually, rescue you!"

To give you a better "feel" for Daniel and what he will go through, I've included a timeline below of Daniel's later acts, visions, and dreams. This timeline in table 8 will help you sort out the book better and may give you reasons to understand Daniel's appeal in this chapter.

Table 8: Visions and Timelines in Daniel	
ca. 600 BC: Dan 2	Nebuchadnezzar's dream of four empires
553 BC: Dan 7	Daniel's first dream of four great beasts (parallel to above)
550 BC: Dan 8	Daniel's second vision of two of the four beasts
539 BC: Dan 5	Handwriting on the wall, fall of Babylon
539 BC: Dan 9	Daniel's prayer of repentance and restoration
539 BC: Dan 9	Prophecy of coming messiah to be cut off
538–36 BC: Dan 10–12	Visions of end times

DANIEL'S THIRD APPEAL: A NON-APPEAL WITH APPEAL

Before Daniel is confronted with the conspiracy we'll see in Dan 6, he has glimpses of God's sovereign rule over people and nations. He got his first inkling of God's sovereign control over history with the prophecies of Isaiah and Jeremiah. Then, he becomes part of the prophecy when he and his friends are taken to Babylon. More detail comes with Nebuchadnezzar's dream of the statue in Dan 2 and the subsequent humiliation and restoration of Nebuchadnezzar in Dan 4. He prophetically interprets the "handwriting on the wall" in Dan 5, and finally, he begins to receive his dreams and visions in Dan 7 and 8. Now, in Dan 6, later in the timeline, he will see God's sovereign control over his life with a new empire: Persia.

At first glance, Daniel's "appeal" will not appear to the reader to be similar to his two previous appeals, first to Ashpenaz and second to Arioch and Nebuchadnezzar. Daniel wisely appealed to his political superiors for an alternative or for some time in each of his two previous appeals. Both appeals serve the purposes of political leadership but are, in a way, compatible with Daniel's faith. In this appeal, however, he says nothing at all. But his silence belies a more profound truth to Daniel's intentions, words, and actions. As in his first two appeals, Daniel looks to God first to determine his sovereign intentions and then to his political superiors to assess their intentions. He does the same here, to good effect. Daniel would have understood from Isa 44:28—45:13 that Darius (Cyrus?) was God's anointed to punish Babylon and liberate the Jews from bondage. Darius was who God had chosen to reign politically. Daniel would also have observed that Darius was trapped by his wise men into making an unalterable law that even he could not break. Daniel chooses to say nothing for good reasons, which we will explore below.

Under Darius as Cyrus, Persia modernized or modified a way to rule a vast empire. This empire dwarfed the Babylonian Empire in land area by an order of magnitude at its peak size and would require significant changes to manage it. Recall that the Babylonian Empire reached a peak of less than .2 million square miles, while Persia reached a peak of well over two million square miles. Persia further developed the institutions of the satrapy that the Medes and Bactrians before him employed but to a much greater extent. Before these reforms, various empires installed vassals, indigenous kings to rule on behalf of the empire, and these kings often revolted against the dominant power or passively but aggressively resisted its wishes. The Persian Empire appointed primarily Persian and Median satraps (i.e., governors) to rule their respective provinces (or satrapy) on behalf of the king. They had wide latitude in governing internally but were indebted to the royal court for foreign and military policy. They were also required to pay taxes and tribute to the central government and to raise troops during war.[9]

Once Persia conquered Babylon, Darius appointed 120 satraps to rule his kingdom, with three administrators over these people. The king appoints Daniel as one of the three. Herodotus records that Persia employed only twenty regional satraps over the entire empire during the reign of Cyrus. So, who are these satraps in this chapter? Given their proximity to the story in Daniel, it seems unlikely they were the provincial satraps (governors) over the far-flung empire. The term satrap was not always used precisely and could be used for officers surrounding the king.[10] Given the context of this passage, it seems likely they are administrators for the headquarters in the kingdom of Babylon, with Daniel and two other senior administrators appointed over them. It was likely, too, that Cyrus employed a combination of Persian and Babylonian people in these positions, with Daniel being the notable exception. These satraps would have likely been the wise men of Babylon and the magi of Persia. And one lone, highly competent, righteous Jew.

The incoming administration must have noted Daniel's reputation, for he was appointed to a senior position early. How did the Persians know of him? The text does not say. Daniel would likely have interacted with several foreign powers, particularly during his long tenure in senior levels of Babylonian service. The Persians recognized Babylonian court intrigue; in fact, many scholars have noted that Persian propaganda played up on the homage of the last king, Nabonidus, to the moon god Sin and not the Babylonian chief god, Marduk.[11] They may have had spies in the court of Belshazzar even as Daniel interpreted the handwriting on the wall for Belshazzar.

But in addition to having a good reputation—likely an outstanding one—Daniel goes further. Daniel 6:3 emphasizes that Daniel distinguished himself among the top three administrators and the other 120 administrators for some time. He continued to perform at a very high level of competence with the skills and wisdom God gave him, but he also must have had integrity and a phenomenal work ethic. Unlike many bureaucrats

---

9. See Waters, *Persia*, 100–103 for a discussion.
10. Kuhurt, "Achaemenid Persian Empire" 114.
11. Oates, *Babylon*, 131–37; and Waters, *Persia*, 43–46.

DANIEL'S THIRD APPEAL: A NON-APPEAL WITH APPEAL

of the ancient world, as in many places today, Daniel held to high ethical standards and did not use his position of power to grow his personal fortune. God continued to grant him favor and compassion in the eyes of his political superiors. He excelled and distinguished himself among the rest of the kingdom officials. Because of this, the king considered making him the prime minister of Babylon.

The satraps and administrators react to the king's intent to promote Daniel. Were these administrators simply jealous of his success? "Who is this foreigner, or who does he think he is?" they may have thought and said. The weak, incompetent, and corrupt will always envy a person of integrity and success and may even feel threatened by them. Even otherwise competent people can envy someone who stands apart from the crowd, as Daniel did.

Or did Daniel somehow threaten these court officials? It seems likely the genesis of the plot to entrap Daniel was because Daniel threatened them by administering the whole palace justly and with integrity. These court officials already had access to the king and likely had developed many ways to profit personally and financially from their positions. Daniel's integrity and work ethic likely threatened their access to the king and their rewards for "gaming" the system to their advantage. From what we know of Daniel, he would have ended their profiting from their official positions.

We don't know how many of these bureaucrats felt this way, but certainly, the number was sufficient to coax the king into a contrived trap for Daniel. A full-blown court intrigue begins to hatch a plan to find fault with Daniel. However, because he was highly competent at administration and ethical in his behavior, this plot could find no accusation of corruption against him. In many ways, the reaction of these court officials recapitulates and emphasizes the opposition of the jealous "wise men" of Babylon against Daniel's three friends in Dan 3.

Daniel had something else against him. He was a Jew. He was not Persian or Mede or even Babylonian. He stood apart from the others. He was also a faithful, pious Jew who consistently kept to his religious practices and would not consort or compromise with the culture around him. We see this particularly in Dan 6:10 when Daniel learns of the plot and goes right on with praying three times a day with open windows toward Jerusalem in a posture of subordination to the God of heaven. The cabal of satraps and administrators sees an opening with Daniel's consistent, overtly religious worship of God, his practices that testified to his worship of the God of heaven. He never hides his subordination to God. They set the trap by ensnaring Darius with a proposal that, to all appearances, looks like something that would honor the king. Of course, honoring the king was the last thing on their minds.

Lastly, Daniel had quickly developed an excellent relationship with the king. After Darius accepts the conspirators' proposal to make it public law that no one is to pray to any person or god other than the king, he is confronted with the fact that Daniel continues to pray to God. The king becomes distressed, likely at both being trapped into making a dumb law and because the law was about to punish a trusted aide, Daniel. Daniel earned Darius's admiration and respect. The king is determined to find a way of escape for Daniel, though none presents itself. His distress at Daniel's fate is further made clear by his hope that Daniel's God can deliver him (v. 16) and his anxiety during the night when he could not eat, be entertained, or sleep (v. 18). The king favored Daniel because of his wisdom, hard work, and subordination to political authority. Daniel never used obsequious flattery or pretenses, like the other officials.

As before, Daniel seeks to understand the facts first before deciding what to do. He may have become familiar with the plot by the way he writes about the event. Did someone else inform him of what the plotters were doing? In v. 7, the conspirators claim that all of the king's officials agreed that the king should issue the decree. It's hard to imagine that every court official, including, as the verse says, "the royal administrators, prefects, satraps, advisers, and governors," were in accord. There were likely many officials who also admired Daniel, including, though we don't know with certainty, his three friends. However, he becomes aware of the plot, perhaps by allies in the bureaucracy. When he learns of the decree, he goes directly home to his upstairs room to the window that faces Jerusalem, and he prays, giving thanks to his God—something he's been doing for a very long time. Did he know the conspirators would be watching him? The text does not say. But, because of the warning about the conspiracy, he may have already been praying to God about the threat of entrapment, and his giving thanks to God was another opportunity for God to demonstrate his sovereign control over events.

Finally, because Daniel has a complete grasp of God's sovereign control over human history, he is more prepared than ever. He now knows to a very high degree of certainty what will come of the nations that rule human history. He knows that God controls the destiny of the gentile nations and individuals within those nations. He would have been intimately familiar

DANIEL'S THIRD APPEAL: A NON-APPEAL WITH APPEAL

with the deliverance of his three friends from the furnace (Dan 3). And he knows that God's kingdom will eventually destroy all human kingdoms. By the time his opponents set the trap, he seems prepared to remain steadfast in the face of political opposition.

The most important part of Daniel's appeal is that he says nothing to the king. He doesn't state the obvious. The king was duped into serving the interests of his court officials by making a law designed to entrap Daniel. He didn't need to tell the king what the king knew when the conspirators confronted him with Daniel's disobedience. The court officials were jealous of Daniel, his possible promotion, and his relationship with the king. The king couldn't show it now, but he was embarrassed. No one likes to be set up or made a fool, especially someone in high political office, either in the modern or ancient world. He would soon demonstrate his rage.

Daniel understood something that we should understand. Because his humility, personal character, political behavior, work ethic, and integrity were all grounded in serving God's kingdom purposes first and political authority second, there could be no legitimate grounds for accusation against him except for his faith. Because he knew this, he also knew he need not respond to this personal attack that threatened his life. The faithful elect of all ages have known and continue to know that their lives may become forfeit in the service of God and his kingdom at any time. He allowed God to defend him and exact vengeance where and when needed in God's good judgment (Deut 32:35; Prov 24:29). He turned the other cheek. He may have implicitly understood that he was blessed because of the persecution of his faith. Even more importantly for his soul, Daniel won't celebrate their fall when the Lord exacts revenge through Darius, indicating his deep love and obedience to God and his word (Prov 24:17–18).

Daniel's appeal without words appeals to us for several reasons. He sought no exemption from the consequences of violating the contrived and unjust law. He doesn't try to use any favor or compassion he has garnered from the king. He doesn't justify or defend himself. In modern, Western terms, we might say, he doesn't stand on his "rights." He doesn't orchestrate a countervailing faction among the court officials. He doesn't blame anyone for anything. Despite the apparent injustice of the decree, Daniel remains respectful and subordinate to the king.

He says nothing throughout the first part of the crisis. Only after he's released from the lion's den by God's deliverance does he show his continued respect for the king and declare his innocence. In vv. 21–22, he says,

"May the king live forever! My God sent his angel, and he shut the mouth of the lions. They have not hurt me, because I was found innocent in his sight. Nor have I ever done any wrong before you, Your Majesty." Furthermore, Daniel seeks no revenge for those who conspired to create the unjust law, nor does he celebrate their judgment when they get thrown into the lions' den for their conspiracy.

Daniel expertly phrased his appeal by remaining silent. Anything he might have said at this point would only have made Darius feel more ridiculous and embarrassed. Anything he would have said would have given joy to his accusers. I'm sure the conspirators were likely waiting to watch Daniel squirm under the threat of death. Yet, he remained silent because nothing could be done. The laws of the Medes and the Persians were irrevocable, even when unjust.

More importantly, any attempt by Daniel to seek an exemption from the law would have untold consequences. Seeking a direct appeal to the king may have established a trend toward rejecting the authority of the laws of the Medes and the Persians. While we may wince at this thought, consider how the Scriptures regard the state's authority. Romans 13:1–5 clearly states the importance of governing authority:

> Let everyone be subject to the governing authorities, for there is no authority except that which God has established. The authorities that exist have been established by God. Consequently, whoever rebels against the authority is rebelling against what God has instituted, and those who do so will bring judgment on themselves. For rulers hold no terror for those who do right, but for those who do wrong. Do you want to be free from fear of the one in authority? Then do what is right and you will be commended. For the one in authority is God's servant for your good. But if you do wrong, be afraid, for rulers do not bear the sword for no reason. They are God's servants, agents of wrath to bring punishment on the wrongdoer. Therefore, it is necessary to submit to the authorities, not only because of possible punishment but also as a matter of conscience.

Paul goes even further in 1 Tim 2:1–2, suggesting that it is incumbent on believers to help the state be ruled well through prayer: "I urge, then, first of all, that requests, prayers, intercession and thanksgiving be made for all people—for kings and all those in authority, that we may live peaceful and quiet lives in all godliness and holiness."

DANIEL'S THIRD APPEAL: A NON-APPEAL WITH APPEAL

The opposite of political authority is political anarchy, the absence of political rule. When this occurs, as can be seen throughout the world today, ungoverned states allow criminal groups, terrorists, and warlords to take over. When they do, civil war erupts, and the weaker of society, usually women and children, pay the heaviest price. Moreover, in the political chaos of failed, failing, and ungoverned states, which we see in many places today, the gospel has little chance of making inroads.

Daniel understood the importance of political authority during his day. He understood that God ordained that Nebuchadnezzar in Babylon would be his instrument in disciplining his remnant of Jews to protect the messianic line. While God disciplined Judah, he did so in such a way as to help the surviving Jews prosper even as they lived as exiles in a hostile land. As Jeremiah wrote to the Jews in exile in Babylon, he also encouraged them to pray for the success of it. Daniel also understood that Persia would eventually conquer and discipline Babylon and that God did this to restore his remnant of the elect to Judah.

Daniel continues to obey political authority. He neither actively nor passively resists the unjust order to be sent to the lion's den. Because he prepared ahead of time and knew the consequences of violating this unjust and contrived law, he understood that the result of continuing to pray publicly would be a sentence of death. Since his early days in Babylonian captivity, he was determined to obey God rather than men, even though his continued submission to God might cost him his life. Ironically, his obedience to God made him a better "employee" of the state.

Daniel does not respond to the king's concern for Daniel's safety, as we see in Dan 6:16: "May your God, whom you serve continually, rescue you." This verse and the following verses, vv. 17–22, make it clear that the king hoped for Daniel's God to rescue him but fretted the whole night about whether God could deliver him. Was Darius only worried about a trusted advisor? Or was he also worried about the administration of his kingdom? From v. 2, we see that the purpose of the three administrators over the satraps was to make them "accountable to [the administrators] so that the king might not suffer loss." Darius would feel his kingdom threatened by Daniel's absence.

By not saying anything, Daniel lets the king see the power of God. He doesn't console the king or explain what God will do. He leaves the king to ruminate over his fate. The king's faith was weak or nonexistent, while

Daniel's was strong. Darius would become further convinced of both the power of God and Daniel's integrity because of Daniel's silence.

In addition, Daniel seeks no changes to the law at any point. He lets the plot play out for all to eventually see the corruption at the heart of the law and the king's susceptibility to flattery. God will be honored and recognized for his sovereign power, Daniel will be recognized for his innocence, the king will become wiser, and the corrupt officials will be given their just desserts. In practical terms, Daniel would likely have a much easier time cleaning up the bureaucracy after their demise.

Further, by disobeying the unjust law and continuing to serve God, Daniel will allow God to demonstrate his power to the court of Darius. The apostle Paul surely knew this, for he does something similar in Acts 16:20–40. In this passage, Paul and Silas were unjustly accused of robbing the livelihood of the owners of the slave girl who was possessed of an unclean spirit. Paul became agitated by her repetition, over the course of many days, of the statement, "These men are servants of the Most High God, who are telling you the way to be saved" (vv. 17–18). He orders the unclean spirit out of her, and he is thrown in jail without a trial. According to Roman law, city officials were first required to sentence Roman citizens by trial. Yet, neither Paul nor Silas say anything of their Roman citizenship until after they are locked up, an earthquake busts open the jail, and the jailer accepts Christ. When the magistrates offer to free Paul and Silas, Paul tells the jailer to have the officials come to release them themselves. This elicits a hurried pardon from the magistrates. Most importantly, Paul's behavior allows God to use the event to bring another person and his family into the kingdom of God.

We see Daniel's mature wisdom in this appeal—a wisdom that is not of this world, a wisdom that comes from a life dedicated to God's kingdom purposes in every situation. Along with his wisdom, Daniel's reputation for integrity and work ethic also get him noticed by the new king early on in his final tour of duty, now with the Medo-Persian Empire in the court of Babylon. Daniel makes himself valuable to the king through his integrity and skill in bureaucratic management, as well as being able to honor the king and the king's domain by his unwillingness to act corruptly.

However, that integrity and skill also elicit hostility from other court officials. They likely saw Daniel threatening their ability to manipulate their jobs for their gain. And because he was a Jew, he was an outsider, not among the "deep state" of his day. But because he was so skilled at his

DANIEL'S THIRD APPEAL: A NON-APPEAL WITH APPEAL

job and because of his integrity, these same court officials could find no grounds for accusation against him, so they had to contrive an unjust law that attacked his faithful dedication to the God of his fathers.

Daniel also thoroughly understood God's sovereign rule over human beings so that he could remain calm in a life-threatening situation. He realized God had sovereign purposes for him and for the kingdoms and kings of which he was a part. In that understanding, Daniel, as he had done before, could look to God's kingdom purposes first and the king's situation second before he decided how to make this appeal with no words. The success of this appeal will soon lead Daniel to be able to make an even higher level appeal to the God of heaven for the release of his people, which we will develop in the next chapter.

7

Daniel's Fourth Appeal: For a Return to the Land

THE YEAR 539 BC brought tumult for Daniel. Daniel recorded four significant events that year that would transform him, his fellow Jews, international politics, and the kingdom of God he served. That year finds Daniel serving high political office, first in the Babylonian Empire's final days and then in the Persian Empire's early days, which are events foreshadowed in Dan 2, 7, and 8. In Dan 5, we saw that he was called out by the ruling faction of Belshazzar's political officers to interpret some strange handwriting on the wall. The evening of the party where Daniel announced the reading of the handwriting and its interpretation foretold of the imminent fall of Babylon and Persia's conquest of it. Babylon did fall, changing the regional political structures of Mesopotamia and the Middle East. Babylon no longer ruled the region of Mesopotamia, the Middle East, and Southeast Asia, but Persia did, an empire an order of magnitude larger than Babylon in geographic scope. The new king, Darius (Dan 6), appointed Daniel to one of the three top administrative posts in the new Babylonian situation, now under the control of the Persian Empire. Two other unnamed people were also appointed to jointly rule with him over all the lesser administrators to hold them accountable for the king's finances. Daniel excelled so greatly in his work that King Darius intended to appoint him over all the administrators soon after, likely because of his outstanding skills and integrity.

Over several months, Daniel's political opponents conspired to entrap and discredit him in the eyes of the new king. Their trap elicits Daniel's

DANIEL'S FOURTH APPEAL: FOR A RETURN TO THE LAND

third appeal, this one without words. God rescued him from the mouth of lions for his faithful conduct. But if that were not enough, Daniel discovered and read a passage from Jeremiah that startled him into prayerful action (Dan 9:2; Jer 25:8–14).

In the first year of Nebuchadnezzar's reign, some sixty-six years before, Jeremiah had prophesied that Judah would be sent into captivity for seventy years. They were to be made captives for the persistent rebellion of the whole society (Jer 25:1–11). By the way Daniel writes in Dan 9:2, he seems to have discovered this prophecy for the first time. Some of Jeremiah's prophecies were sent to Babylon, where Daniel could have read them. Jeremiah 29, for example, is an open letter to the Jewish exiles who live in Babylon, where the prophet encourages them in order to help them understand how to prosper by serving Babylon. Jeremiah 29:10 refers to the seventy years first prophesied in Jer 25. The Scriptures are silent about why Daniel hadn't read this prophecy until now. Perhaps he had read it earlier, but it wasn't salient for him then. Now, it is. As a result of the persistent rebellions of Jews in their homeland leading to subsequent campaigns by Nebuchadnezzar to subdue Judah, destroy the temple, and deport many thousands of Jews back to Babylon, Daniel likely realized that his people had yet to repent of their ways.

Daniel understands from reading the book of Jeremiah that the terminus for the seventy years of exile is drawing close. From Ezra 1:1–4, we learn that Cyrus gave the edict to restore Babylon's captives to their original homeland in 538 BC, in the second year of his conquest. Historically, some Jewish exiles began their return that year, but the full return didn't happen for many years. The Ezra passage hints at the reluctance of some to return.

To determine the end of the seventy years of exile, we must determine when the exile began. Was it 605 BC with the deportation of Daniel and his three friends? If so, then only sixty-seven years would have passed. Or was it later, with the first large deportation of 597, or even later, with the biggest one of 586, when Nebuchadnezzar destroyed the temple? If so, then it would likely have been an even shorter period.

Several hypotheses have been suggested for the different dates for Jeremiah's prophecy. The first is that the seventy years was a *rough* timeline for the prophecy.[1] While Daniel and his three friends were taken in 605, the largest deportation didn't occur until 586 with the destruction of the temple. So, the alternative is that the dates should correspond with the temple

---

1. Pierce, "Spiritual Failure," 216.

destruction of 586 and the second temple's rebuilding completion in 516.[2] But this fails to explain why Daniel understood its terminus around the time of his prayer in 539. The first hypothesis ignores the explicit mention of seventy years. One scholar suggests that the exile begins with Josiah's death in 608, making it exactly seventy years to the time Cyrus issues the edict.[3] Still, no reason is given for this date except that it makes the seventy years work precisely.

There may be another explanation. Habakkuk 1 may help us here. Habakkuk's prophecy was likely written between 609 and 605 BC, after the death of the last righteous king, Josiah. This would have also been about the time when Nebuchadnezzar began conquering Palestine. In this passage, the prophet laments the shameless robbery and oppression of the common people in Judah by the nobles. In Hab 1:2–4, the prophet says: "How long, O Lord, must I call for help, but you do not listen? Or cry out to you, 'Violence!' but you do not save? Why do you make me look at injustice? Why do you tolerate wrongdoing? Destruction and violence are before me; there is strife, and conflict abounds. Therefore the law is paralyzed, and justice never prevails. The wicked hem in the righteous, so that justice is perverted."

Gleason Archer, a prominent Old Testament scholar, notes that Habakkuk's lament had to be about the "corrupt and rapacious nobles, allied with corrupt religious leaders" who were using the courts to oppress and rob the poor, as "it was the nobility that were first taken into captivity in the two preliminary deportations of 605 and 597. The majority of the lower classes were left in the land until the third deportation of 586."[4] Daniel and his friends were in the first deportation of the nobility in 605.

It seems likely, therefore, that the period of seven decades begins with Daniel's deportation, with its terminus at the edict of Cyrus in 538. If so, a better explanation may fit the data, indicating less than seventy years of captivity. Daniel's prayer of restoration that begins with reading the prophecy of Jeremiah (roughly 539 BC) *precipitates* God's sovereign actions in history, which Jeremiah prophesied would occur in 536 BC. Daniel takes agency by beginning the process through prayer. God moved the heart of King Cyrus to announce his edict to restore the deported people a couple of years ahead of time. However, the complete fulfillment of that restoration

---

2. See Archer, *Survey*, 370–71.
3. Gentry, "Daniel's Seventy Weeks," 32.
4. Archer, *Survey*, 365.

DANIEL'S FOURTH APPEAL: FOR A RETURN TO THE LAND

takes many years, decades, and even centuries. Many Jews never left Babylon, and many others dispersed to other areas, including Persia, Egypt, and the regions of modern Arabia.[5]

Daniel's reading of Jeremiah's prophecy compelled him to return to the Scriptures. Daniel clearly understood the requirements of the covenantal relationship between God and Israel from the Mosaic law. Leviticus 26 lays out the consequences of obedience and disobedience to God's divine laws for living in proper relation to him. It's not intended to be a punitive decree but rather a loving encouragement to Israel to follow God with all their hearts and to live well with him. There is an exquisite sequence to the blessings of obedience (Lev 26:6–13) and the discipline for disobedience (Lev 26:14–39). God will increasingly bless his peoples' obedience and bring discipline to restore his people to proper relations. The penultimate disciplinary action will remove them from the land to get their attention and allow it to rest. Recall that ten of the original twelve tribes of Israel have already been destroyed by Assyria over one hundred years before. Judah (consisting of the two tribes of Judah and Benjamin) was the last remnant of the people God called out from the disenfranchised human race (Gen 12). God jealously guards his promises.

The final section (Lev 26:40–45)[6] offers the way to return to obedience and blessing:

> But if they will confess their sins and the sins of their ancestors—their unfaithfulness and their hostility toward me, which made me hostile toward them so that I sent them into the land of their enemies—then when their uncircumcised hearts are humbled and they pay for their sin, I will remember my covenant with Jacob and my covenant with Isaac and my covenant with Abraham, and I will remember the land. For the land will be deserted by them and will enjoy its sabbaths while it lies desolate without them. They will pay for their sins because they rejected my laws and abhorred my decrees. Yet in spite of this, when they are in the land of their enemies, I will not reject them or abhor them so as to destroy them completely, breaking my covenant with them. I am the LORD their God. But for their sake I will remember the covenant with their ancestors whom I brought out of Egypt in the sight of the nations to be their God. I am the LORD.

---

5. Bruce, *Israel*, 99–115. See also, Rabinovich, "Exiled." Rabinovich points out from archaeological findings that the Jews were one of only two peoples exiled to Babylonia to have returned to their homeland, though it is unknown what percentage returned.

6. See also Deut 28:15–68 and 30:1–10.

A companion passage in Deut 30:1–10 also instructs faithful believers on seeking restoration with God and the land after exile. Daniel knew what God would need to restore the exiles back to Judah. God will discipline them while unconditionally keeping a remnant of people faithful to him.

THE APPEAL

In the first year of Darius son of Xerxes (a Mede by descent), who was made ruler over the Babylonian kingdom—in the first year of his reign, I, Daniel, understood from the Scriptures, according to the word of the Lord given to Jeremiah the prophet, that the desolation of Jerusalem would last seventy years. So I turned to the Lord and pleaded with him in prayer and petition, in fasting, and in sackcloth and ashes.

I prayed to the Lord my God and confessed:

"Lord, the great and awesome God, who keeps his covenant of love with all who love him and keep his commandments, we have sinned and done wrong. We have been wicked and have rebelled; we have turned away from your commands and laws. We have not listened to your servants the prophets, who spoke in your name to our kings, our princes and our ancestors, and to all the people of the land.

"Lord, you are righteous, but this day we are covered with shame—the people of Judah and the inhabitants of Jerusalem and all Israel, both near and far, in all the countries where you have scattered us because of our unfaithfulness to you. We and our kings, our princes and our ancestors are covered with shame because we have sinned against you. The Lord our God is merciful and forgiving, even though we have rebelled against him; we have not obeyed the Lord our God or kept the laws he gave us through his servants the prophets. All Israel has transgressed your law and turned away, refusing to obey you.

"Therefore the curses and sworn judgments written in the Law of Moses, the servant of God, have been poured out on us, because we have sinned against you. You have fulfilled the words spoken against us and against our rulers by bringing on us great disaster. Under the whole heaven nothing has even been done like what has been done to Jerusalem. Just as it is written in the Law of Moses, all this disaster has come on us, yet we have not sought the favor of the Lord our God by turning from our sins and giving attention to your truth. The Lord did not hesitate to bring the disaster upon us, for the Lord our God is righteous in everything he does; yet we have not obeyed him.

"Now, Lord our God, who brought your people out of Egypt with a mighty hand and who made for yourself a name that endures to this day, we have sinned, we have done wrong. Lord, in keeping with all your righteous acts, turn away your anger and your wrath from Jerusalem, your city, your holy hill. Our sins and the iniquities of our ancestors have made Jerusalem and your people an object of scorn to all those around us.

"Now, our God, hear the prayers and petitions of your servant. For your sake, Lord, look with favor on your desolate sanctuary. Give ear, our God, and hear; open your eyes and see the desolation of the city that bears your Name. We do not make requests of you because we are righteous, but because of your great mercy. Lord, listen! Lord, forgive! Lord, hear and act! For your sake, my God, do not delay, because your city and your people bear your Name."
(Dan 9:1–19)

There is much overlap between Daniel's prayer of repentance and restoration with the Leviticus passage cited above. Daniel confesses his sins, the sins of the fathers, and the sins of his fellow Jews. He confesses the rebellion and iniquity that led God to the penultimate form of discipline for his people: forced military conquest and deportation to a foreign land. Daniel humbly appeals to God's mercy for deliverance as he delivered Israel from Egypt many centuries before. But there is more.

Daniel likely also paid attention to Solomon's temple dedication and the Levitical laws. In 1 Kgs 8:23–53, Solomon lists the conditions of the dedication, which include how and where to pray to the temple for repentance and restoration. Remember while you read this passage that Babylon will destroy Solomon's temple in 586 BC.

In 1 Kgs 8:23–31 and 46–53, Solomon stands before the alter and says:

> Lord, God of Israel, there is no God like you in heaven above or on earth below—you who keep your covenant of love with your servants who continue wholeheartedly in your way. You have kept your promise to your servant David my father; with your mouth you have promised and with your hand you have fulfilled it—as it is today.
>
> Now Lord, God of Israel, keep for your servant David my father the promises you made to him when you said, "You shall never fail to have a successor sit before me on the throne of Israel, if only your descendants are careful in all they do to walk before

me faithfully as you have done." And now, God of Israel, let your word that you promised your servant David my father come true.

But will God really dwell on earth? The heavens, even the highest heaven, cannot contain you. How much less this temple I have built! Yet give attention to your servant's prayer and his plea for mercy, Lord my God. Hear the cry and the prayer that your servant is praying in your presence this day. May your eyes be open toward this temple night and day, this place of which you said, "My Name shall be there," so that you will hear the prayer your servant prays toward this place. Hear the supplication of your servant and of your people Israel when they pray toward this place. Hear from heaven, your dwelling place, and when you hear, forgive. . . .

When they sin against you—for there is no one who does not sin—and you become angry with them and give them over to their enemies, who take them captive to their own land, far away or near; and if they have a change of heart in the land where they are held captive, and repent and plead with you in the land of their captors and say, "We have sinned, we have done wrong, we have acted wickedly"; and if they turn back to you with all their heart and soul in the land of the enemies who took them captive, and pray to you toward the land you gave their ancestors, toward the city you have chosen and the temple I have built for your Name; then from heaven, your dwelling place, hear their prayer and their plea, and uphold their cause. And forgive your people who have sinned against you; forgive all the offenses they have committed against you, and cause their captors to show them mercy; for they are your people and your inheritance, whom you brought out of Egypt, out of that iron-smelting furnace.

May your eyes be open to your servant's plea and to the plea of your people Israel, and may you listen to them whenever they cry out to you. For you singled them out from all the nations of the world to be your own inheritance, just as you declared through your servant Moses when you, Sovereign Lord, brought our ancestors out of Egypt.

Comparing the three passages of Lev 26:14–46, Solomon's temple dedication in 1 Kgs 8:23–53, and Daniel's prayer in Dan 9:1–23 may prove helpful.

All three passages state or imply several things in common and some unique things. First, all three passages appeal to God, who brought his people out of the land of Egypt. God had first given Israel his inheritance out of all the nations of the earth. Later, God delivered his people, who had been enslaved for over four hundred years by the superpower of the day,

Egypt. That deliverance remained a seminal event in Jewish history (and remains so today). The Passover ceremony ensures that the bitterness of captivity, faithfulness, and power of God will not be forgotten. What God did then, he could do again. (The reminder in these prayers antedates that ceremony.)

Of the three passages, only Leviticus explicitly states that God will leave a remnant of his people even under extreme conditions of discipline that could include captivity (Lev 26:44). However, both Solomon, in his temple dedication, and Daniel, in his prayer, assume God leaves a remnant, or there would be no hope for a prayer of repentance and restoration. Solomon and Daniel knew and understood that if they or God's people were still alive, God would likely give them a chance at restoration.

Since the Levitical passage did not assume the presence of a temple as it did not yet exist, the passage does not suggest that God's people should pray toward Jerusalem in general or the temple in particular. But Solomon makes it important to pray toward the temple when they have been defeated by an enemy (vv. 33–34) and toward Jerusalem and the temple when God's people are held captive in foreign lands (vv. 46–49). Solomon knows too well that God could discipline rebellious Israelites through conquest and enslavement by gentile nations (Lev 26:33; 1 Kgs 8:46–48; Dan 9:7). Solomon's injunction likely explains why Daniel made it his practice to open the western windows of his apartment and pray three times a day toward Jerusalem and the desolate sanctuary (Dan 6:20, 9:17). There was no requirement in the Mosaic law to do so. Still, Solomon makes it a critical point in his dedication. Solomon and Daniel understood that God doesn't reside in his temple (1 Kgs 8:27, 30) but in heaven, where he answers prayers.

Solomon and Daniel call God's covenant with Israel his "covenant of love" (1 Kgs 8:23; Dan 9:4). The term covenant of love denotes the special relationship God first established with his chosen people. All gentile nations rebelled against God at the Tower of Babel by trying to make a name (shem) for themselves instead of relying on the power of his Name (shem).[7] Because of their rebellion, he disinherited them by scattering them to the four winds (Gen 11:1–9) to be ruled over by foreign gods (Deut 32:8–9; Ps 82).[8] Only then does God call forth his portion from among the nations

---

7. In biblical literature, especially among Jews, *ha-shem* or "the Name" is often substituted for Jehovah. The Name often is used as a substitute for the person of God. See Heiser, *Unseen Realm*, 115, 145.

8. For a good technical discussion of this, see Heiser, *Unseen Realm*, chs. 14, 30.

through Abram (later, Abraham; Gen 12). It is through Abraham that God begins his covenant relationship with his chosen people.

Daniel had prepared himself thoroughly for this appeal. Since the beginning of his captivity, likely before, Daniel habituated himself to a life well lived in light of God's laws and requirements. Daniel did more than obey the overt rituals of the law; he obeyed faithfully from his whole heart. He paid attention to the Scriptures he had access to and learned from them how to live a life of faith and trust in God and in God's direction for his life. Early in his career, he committed to his small fellowship of righteous friends supporting each other with prayer and petitions for one another and the challenges they would face. The prayerful support of his three friends helped him discern the nature and interpretation of Nebuchadnezzar's dream in Dan 2, which confounded the king's court magicians. Daniel and his friends also excelled at the king's service, vastly outperforming the other elite children Babylon had taken captive and placed in the three-year study program.

Daniel was known for his righteousness and right living. He lives in such a way as to glorify God and highlight God's sovereign rule from the heavens among gentile kings and officials, even those that despise God. In addition to all the other challenges and blessings he goes through during his time in Babylon and early Persia, the angel Gabriel calls him "highly esteemed" in Dan 9:23. Ezekiel elevates Daniel alongside Noah and Job as among the top three most righteous people living (Ezek 14:14, 20).

Daniel faithfully works at discerning Scriptures relevant to interpreting his era's politics. Ezekiel regards Daniel as wise beyond compare (Ezek 28:3). In addition to studying Scriptures and living faithfully to God through habitual prayer, Daniel developed wisdom to discern how God moves through history to accomplish his kingdom purposes during his day. That's not as easy as it sounds, for many "false" prophets argued for very different things while Daniel was alive. Put into our context, there was a cacophony of voices and narratives about what was going on. His version of the competition between CNN, Fox News, other major stations and newspapers, many sermons from various traditions, and modern social media would have produced as much noise about what God was up to in history as we experience in our day. Whose narrative did Daniel trust? Whose narrative do you trust? Fighting through human-sponsored narratives takes much work through prayer, Scripture reading, and thoughtful inquiry.

DANIEL'S FOURTH APPEAL: FOR A RETURN TO THE LAND

As we saw earlier, Daniel likely understood from Isa 49:6 that he could take "agency" during his time of captivity to become a light for the gentiles into whose hands he was put in subjection. He could be ready when he discerned the need to make wise appeals, such as when he chose to appeal for a vegetarian diet that would allow him and his friends to remain "set apart" from the other captives (Dan 1). He could be ready when Nebuchadnezzar needed someone to interpret a fearful dream (Dan 2). He could be both ready and bold enough to tell a king he admired and respected (Dan 4) what his dream portended for the king's arrogance toward God's sovereign rule over politics. He boldly tells another king, Belshazzar (Dan 5), that his empire is doomed because of his reckless disregard for God's temple objects. He could also discern when to stay silent, when speaking would only embarrass still another king (Dan 6). He fully integrated his faith life and work life into a seamless whole. Daniel lived righteously and faithfully during his captivity without evincing any self-righteousness in his words and conduct.

Daniel stayed alert to God's sovereign movement through history. By example, he challenges us to be prepared to understand how God sovereignly moves throughout our history in our country and the world. While you may say that Daniel had the prophecies of Jeremiah and Isaiah to guide him during his day, few of his contemporaries paid nearly as close attention to them and determined how they applied to themselves. We, too, have Scriptures that are helpful for us today. Our core mission statement is found in Matt 28:19—that is, to make disciples throughout the world to reverse the disinheritance of the gentiles that began after the Tower of Babel and to expand the kingdom of God. First Peter 3:15–16 tells us the way we are to do it with our neighbors—that is, with gentleness and respect. The question remains: Are we staying ready to discern God's sovereign moves today through our righteous living, study of Scriptures, openness to God in prayer, and reading of how God is acting in international politics? We see the gospel spreading worldwide and meeting fierce resistance in many parts of Asia, the 10/40 window,[9] and the Middle East. Our mission remains an unfinished task. Can we discern how our day's international politics may help or hinder the spread of the gospel? Are we investing wisely to help the gospel spread?

---

9. The 10/40 window refers to the region of the eastern hemisphere and the western region of North Africa, the Middle East, and Asia between 10 and 40 degrees north of the equator, where the gospel has had the least impact. See Joshua Project, "What Is the 10/40 Window?."

While that remains our general mission, the specific mission for each of us will differ. Like Daniel, God has placed us in unique settings, with unique families, upbringings, education, churches, and our country. God doesn't make everyone a Daniel in the sense of serving in high political office in foreign lands; he does, however, have sovereign purposes for each one of us in our particular settings. Like Daniel, we are to take "agency" and determine how best to use our gifts, talents, and circumstances to help God's kingdom purposes here and now.

Daniel's appeal appealed to God for a variety of reasons. Daniel states the objective truth. He explicitly appeals to God's character and past actions that have kept the remnant of his inheritance alive. He notes God keeps his covenant of love for those who love him (9:4). Righteousness belongs to God alone (9:7, 14). Daniel sees both compassion and forgiveness as fundamental to God's character (9:9). He believes God faithfully keeps his word (9:12). He compares God's character and faithfulness to human faithlessness and rebellion (9:5–11). He also understands that God's faithfulness doesn't merely reside in being blessed as a people but also in being disciplined when they disobey his covenant of love (9:11–14). They received the natural consequences of their disobedience.

Daniel doesn't say these things to flatter God as if God could be flattered. Humans constantly flatter other people, mainly to get something from them. Humans sinfully use flattery to grease the wheels in pursuing their interests. But God will have none of that.

For comparison, take a look at Acts 24:1–4. In this passage, the lawyer Tertullus uses flattery on behalf of the high priest Ananias to get the apostle Paul convicted before the governor Felix. He flatters the governor in ways that are patent nonsense. Verses 2–3 record this appeal of Tertullus: "When Paul was called in, Tertullus presented his case before Felix: 'We have enjoyed a long period of peace under you and your foresight has brought about reforms in this nation. Everywhere and in every way, most excellent Felix, we acknowledge this with profound gratitude.'"

The historian Tacitus regarded Antoninus Felix as a cruel, base, and dishonorable man. He had a sexual relationship with Drusilla, making her husband a cuckold, to get a new wife for himself. Acts 24:26 records that he looked to Paul not to hear the gospel as much as to receive a bribe and unjustly confined him for two years in the hope that one would be forthcoming. Corruption and crime increased during Felix's governorship, and he was recalled to Rome, where Nero acquitted him after Felix's brother appealed.[10] As Paul discussed the gospel, Felix grew afraid of the implications of failing to live a righteous life and of the coming judgment and sent Paul away. Felix was not the man Tertullus said he was. Tertullus flattered the governor by saying what he thought the governor wanted to hear to get what he wanted from him.

On the other hand, Daniel accurately believes what he prays in this chapter. Like Paul does before Felix, Daniel states the facts plainly. Daniel neither blames God for Judah's rebellion nor the consequences of Judah's rebellion. He assumes responsibility for the catastrophes that have occurred to Judah and to himself in particular. Daniel includes his confession of sin and the sin of his people and its leaders in his prayer, acknowledging what Solomon said before, "for there is no one who does not sin" (1 Kgs 8:46). Daniel likely was looking for a way out of this catastrophe for his people. Reading this passage in Jeremiah, he found a justifiable way to petition God actively.

Daniel is no fatalist, however. Like so many of us may be tempted to do, he could have reasoned that God will do what he will do in his way and time. Jeremiah's prophecy foretold an end to the troubles in seventy years, and Daniel would have known God would bring about his promise within several years. But Daniel took "agency" and initiated this prayer of repentance and restoration. As he has done throughout the book, he engages God through prayer and study, and God engages him through visions, dreams, interpretations, and, occasionally, celestial visitors. And in this case, God deliberately answers him. Daniel prays, and God moves Cyrus's heart to issue the decree to let the Jews return home (Ezra 1:1–4; Prov 21:1), even though Cyrus does not acknowledge God. In this way, Daniel's relationship with God is contingent: God loves, Daniel obeys, and God responds in love to Daniel's obedience.

Daniel behaves in a way that increases his appeal. As we said above, Daniel does none of the following to manipulate God, were that even possible. He engages in behaviors and practices that enhance his fitness to petition God on behalf of his fellow countrymen and to receive the special revelations he will get after he prays for repentance and restoration. He first turns his attention to God through prayer and supplications (9:3). The Hebrew word here for prayer means intercessory prayer. He intercedes on behalf of his fellow Jews in Babylon, those who remain in Judah, and those

---

10. Tacitus, *Histories*, 277.

scattered elsewhere.[11] While Hebrew has over a dozen words for prayer, this word is found seventy-six times in the Old Testament and mainly in the Psalms (some thirty-two times). Several Psalms have superscriptions about this word, prayer, including Pss 17, 86, 90, 102, and 142 (NIV). This word for intercessory prayer is some form of appeal to God for assistance, usually referring to God's previous acts of kindness, compassion, righteousness, and his name.[12]

Supplications differ from prayer but complement it. The Hebrew word for supplications means to beseech, implore, and entreat. They are less formal entreaty than the outpourings of a troubled soul.[13] Supplications are also associated with weeping in Jer 3:21 and 31:9.

Daniel's supplications are many throughout his prayer. He requests God to "hear the prayers and supplications of his servant" (9:17). He asks God to "give ear, and hear" and to open his eyes and "see the desolation" of the city that "bears your name" (v. 18). He implores God to "listen," to "forgive," and to "hear and act" (v. 19).

Daniel indicates in v. 3 that he does other things as well. He also fasts and covers himself with sackcloth and ashes while appealing to God with prayer and supplications. Fasting is an outward act denoting the inward reality. It is the intentional deprivation of nourishment as a sign that one is experiencing great sorrow, as a means to gain God's attention, and to seek his righteousness. Fasting is usually done for several reasons, including to mourn over sins and seek righteousness in one's life or community before a critical decision or after an ominous turn of events. Ashes are associated with mourning over death or sin, and the wearing of sackcloth is used as a garment of grief and self-abasement. When worn by the prophets Elijah and John the Baptist, the sackcloth required a call to trembling and repentance (2 Kgs 1:8; Matt 3:4).

Daniel lays out the problem in precise detail. He compares God's character with the character and failings of his people, which led to the disaster that came upon Judah. Throughout his prayer, Daniel identifies several characteristics of God, which we would label today as "attributes," an idea

---

11. A sizeable number of Jews fled Judah to Egypt and established a community in the upper Nile, near Elephantine. Some of the papyri, appropriately called Elephantine Papyri, have survived through the centuries, giving a picture of life in self-imposed exile. Jewish tradition holds that the prophet Jeremiah was taken there, but no specific proof exists that he did. See Archer, *Survey*, 369.

12. Harris et al., *Theological Workbook*, 725–26.

13. Harris et al., *Theological Workbook*, 304.

DANIEL'S FOURTH APPEAL: FOR A RETURN TO THE LAND

that would have been foreign to an ancient Jew. The ancients did not look at God abstractly; instead, they would have looked at these characteristics as relational ones, as describing a covenantal relationship between God, who loves his people, and a people who return God's love with faithlessness and rebellion. Daniel says God is faithful (v. 4), righteous (v. 7), merciful and forgiving (vv. 8, 18), powerful (v. 15), and wrathful toward faithlessness (v. 16).

Daniel brutally details his failings and the failings of his people toward God and his covenant of love. Everyone has sinned against God, which means to have missed the mark or the way, the goal or standard God set for his people. By this, Daniel means that all of Judah failed to find the way of God in their dealings with him and with other people.[14] He and his people did this by doing wrong or committing iniquity, which means they bent, twisted, or distorted what God said or promised.[15] They had become wicked, which means in their lifestyle they were both hostile to God and hostile to their community.[16] Living this way, they ruptured relationships with God and their community through unrighteous behavior. Earlier, we saw how Habakkuk depicted those broken relationships, mainly by the wealthy political and religious leaders using the courts to exploit the poor among them. Finally, Daniel points out that they rebelled, which means abrogating or nullifying a covenant relationship. The vassal of this covenant, Judah, literally abrogated God's loving relationship with them by doing all these things.

For these reasons, Daniel prays humbly. He knows that neither he nor his fellow Jews have any grounds for requesting anything from God at this point. He can only appeal to God based on God's past behavior and actions of mercy. Daniel also appeals to God because his people and desolate sanctuary bear his name. He, like us, can only fall on the mercy of God.

Daniel continued throughout his life in Babylon to remain subordinate to all political and divine authority. Daniel does not tell us in chapter 9 whether he took some time off from his regular duties to study the Jeremiah prophecy and to begin fasting and praying for repentance and restoration. He does indicate that in the third year of the reign of Cyrus, king of Persia (two years after this), Daniel says that he took three weeks for his fast and prayers (Dan 10:2–3). We may surmise with reasonable confidence that Daniel did his fast and prayer in this chapter within his allotted "free" time

---

14. Harris et al., *Theological Workbook*, 277.
15. Harris et al., *Theological Workbook*, 656.
16. Harris et al., *Theological Workbook*, 863.

away from his official duties and did not abuse his position of power and authority for his private activities.

However, the main thing to note about Daniel's submissiveness in this appeal is that he never presumes any righteousness on his part. Instead, he fully identifies with all the sins of his people, including kings, princes, ancestors, and his fellow Jews. God repeatedly sent his prophets to every stratum of society in Judah. Daniel lists all the failings of God's people, including their sin, iniquity, wickedness, and rebellion. He identifies with Judah's failings using the first-person plural (we) throughout when comparing Judah's sins and failings with God's relational characteristics.

Neither does Daniel flatter God. Daniel appeals to God from a whole, undivided heart. He states the truth and is mindful of the harm such failings have on the people's relationship with God and one another. He argues correctly that God rightly blesses those who obey him and shows how he and Judah deserved the discipline God inflicted on them through this captivity. Throughout, Daniel remains faithful to the requirements of the Mosaic law and the requirements for the prayer of repentance and restoration. Daniel indeed is not only "light to the Gentiles" but someone who brings about the "restoration of Jacob" (Isa 49:6). Daniel subordinated himself to God's call for him to remain his servant through difficult times.

THE ANSWER(S)

As we've indicated above, God answered Daniel's prayer very quickly. Within a year, the Persian king Cyrus announced the mandate to allow people held captive by Babylon to return home. Ezra 4:1–4 records the king's decree in Aramaic, the *lingua franca* of the day. There are several alternative explanations for how long the seventy years were—whether it was *roughly* seventy years or we must adjust the dates to make them work. On the other hand, it could be that Daniel's prayer precipitates God's sovereign move in history. We don't know with a high degree of certainty. Still, we know that most of Judah did not repent along with Daniel.[17] Did it only take the prayer of one righteous man to trigger God's sovereign move, or was God waiting for at least one to begin the process?

Daniel gets another answer, one he could not have anticipated. As his prayer and fast conclude, the angel Gabriel interrupts him at the evening

---

17. Pierce argues that their failure to repent led the seventy-year exile to be extended to the seventy weeks of exile. See "Spiritual Failure," 219–20.

DANIEL'S FOURTH APPEAL: FOR A RETURN TO THE LAND

sacrifice to give him new information—another revelation—this time of what is to come for his people (Dan 9:20–27). Gabriel, who appeared to Daniel in Dan 8 to explain the vision of a ram and a goat (the empires of Persia and Greece), interrupts Daniel's prayer to inform Daniel of something urgent and long range for his people (vv. 24–27):

> Seventy "sevens" are decreed for your people and your holy city to finish transgression, to put an end to sin, to atone for wickedness, to bring in everlasting righteousness, to seal up vision and prophecy and to anoint the Most Holy Place.
>
> Know and understand this: From the issuing of the decree to restore and rebuild Jerusalem until the Anointed One, the ruler, comes, there will be seven "sevens," and sixty-two "sevens." It will be rebuilt with streets and a trench, but in times of trouble. After the sixty-two "sevens," the Anointed One will be put to death and will have nothing. The people of the ruler who will come will destroy the city and the sanctuary. The end will come like a flood: War will continue until the end, and desolations have been decreed. He will confirm a covenant with the many for one "seven." In the middle of the "seven" he will put an end to sacrifice and offering. And at the temple, he will set up an abomination that causes desolation, until the end that is decreed is poured out on him.

By the grammar of the text, it looks like there is a total of seventy "sevens," understood by conservative Christian and Jewish scholars as seventy weeks of years, equaling a total of 490 years. These seventy "sevens" are divided into three groups: the first seven "sevens" of forty-nine years, the sixty-two "seven" of 434 years, and the final seven of seven years.

There are three conservative Christian schools of thought about this revelation. For lack of better terms, I have labeled them the preterist, the messianic, and the messianic plus tribulation schools. The preterist view holds that because most Jews did not repent of their sin and rebellion toward God near the end of the Babylonian captivity, their seventy years of captivity extended to seventy weeks of years (i.e., 490 years) starting with the reign of Nebuchadnezzar through the eras of the Persians and the Greeks. This view holds that the end of these 490 years occurs "neither during the Greek nor Roman occupations, but rather at the zenith of Israel's independence under the Hasmonean kings Arisotobulus I (104–3 BC) and his half-brother Alexander Jannaeus (103–76 BC)."[18] It is a less traditional conservative view.

---

18. Pierce, "Spiritual Failure," 212.

The more traditional school of thought (messianic plus tribulation) is that the 483 years lead up to the birth, ministry, and death of Jesus the Messiah on behalf of human beings and the subsequent destruction of Jerusalem and the temple. The remaining week of seven years occurs during "end times" when the tribulation, the final seven years of human history before the millennial reign of Christ, occurs.[19] The messianic view, which is a less traditional but still conservative school, holds that the final week of seven years is when the "Anointed One will be put to death and have nothing" referring, of course, to the sacrificial death of Jesus Christ on the cross and the subsequent destruction of Jerusalem that followed.[20]

While it may be a little disconcerting that, even with twenty-twenty hindsight, conservative scholarship cannot fix the interpretation of Daniel's seventy weeks of years, the more profound message had its intended effect. There is strong historical evidence that different Jewish schools of thought also believed the messiah would come sometime during Jesus' ministry. These schools of thought included the Essenes, the Pharisees, and the Zealots.[21] That is to say, the intended message of hope for the coming of the messiah, the coming solution for the problem of sin, and the inauguration of the kingdom of God happened within the timeframe of expectations that Gabriel's revelation of the seventy weeks of years would have occurred. Only when he did not come (in Jewish thinking) did these schools of thought reinterpret the prophecy as non-messianic.[22] Christian thinkers picked up the messianic interpretation where Jewish scholars left off.

Interestingly, however, all interpretations of Daniel's seventy weeks have something in common. They are remarkably detailed in their understanding of the timeline for the coming messiah, even with the ambiguity of the prophecy. The sole exception to this is the preterist view mentioned above. One scholar notes, "There is a curious contrast between the imprecision of the figures in the 70-week prophecy and the over-precision in all of its old interpreters, Jewish and Christian alike, from the second century BC onwards." We will see and examine how this plays out with Daniel's final appeal in the next chapter, where he appeals for greater clarity on the next installment of the apocalyptic revelation he will soon receive.

---

19. Archer, *Encyclopedia*, 289–92.
20. Gentry, "Daniel's Seventy Weeks," 37.
21. For a detailed evaluation of the evidence, see Beckwith, "Daniel 9," 521–42.
22. Beckwith, "Daniel 9," 536.

8

Daniel's Fifth Appeal: More Information

AS WE MENTIONED EARLIER, the book of Daniel has more apocalypses (revelations) than any other book of the Bible, except the book of Revelation. These revelations were not only given to Daniel, whom Jesus refers to as a prophet. The first apocalypse was given to the pagan king Nebuchadnezzar in Dan 2. In that chapter, written in Aramaic, the king had a dream that frightened him so greatly that he was about to slay all the wise men of Babylon for their inability to tell him the dream and interpret it. Though Nebuchadnezzar received the vision from God, he neither remembered the dream nor understood it. All the wise men Nebuchadnezzar had threatened to kill included Daniel and his three friends. However, Daniel successfully appealed to the king for time to respond, and he appealed to the God of heaven to understand what the king dreamed and how to interpret that dream. He likely made these appeals in about 602 BC.

In Dan 2, God revealed to Daniel that the king's vision was of a mighty statue. That statue depicted a head of gold, breast and arms of silver, a belly and thighs of bronze, and legs of iron, as well as having toes of iron mixed with baked clay. Daniel was given the interpretation of this statue, representing four successive empires that would occur throughout history and a fifth empire that would be made without human help, God's kingdom. The four empires were, first, the head of gold depicting Babylon itself; second, the breast and arms of silver, depicting the Medo-Persian Empire; third, the belly and thighs of bronze, depicting the Macedonian (Greek) Empire; and fourth, the legs of iron and toes of iron and clay, depicting the Empire of Rome out into the future. The final (fifth) kingdom, represented by stone, would start small and eventually overwhelm the last human kingdom with God's power. Daniel established his credibility with the king, who honored Daniel with a promotion. He also gains credibility with Jewish sages, for Deut 18:21–22 avers that a prophet is not to be seen as commissioned by God if the thing he predicts fails to happen. For this reason, Jewish religious scholars included the book of Daniel in their inspired, canonical works.

Nearly fifty years later, in approximately 553 BC, Daniel had his first vision during the first year of Babylonian king Belshazzar (Dan 7). He records this vision in Aramaic, as it pertains to the general outline of history for Jews and gentiles alike. In his vision, he sees four great and mighty beasts that parallel and expand on Nebuchadnezzar's vision in his dream of the statue; it, too, finishes with a kingdom given by the Ancient of Days to the "son of man" coming on clouds. The four beasts are, in turn, the lion (Babylon), the bear (Medo-Persia), the leopard (Macedonia), and the final, most terrifying and powerful beast (Rome), which is unlike any animal. This final beast has ten horns. Another little horn sprouts during this fourth empire and uproots three other horns. Conservative scholars have noted that this fourth empire extends well beyond the original period of the Roman Republic and Roman Empire into the future, even for us. In his vision, Daniel turns and witnesses a divine council of God that pronounces judgment on this fourth and last empire before handing over dominion to the son of man to establish the kingdom of God on earth. Daniel turns to one of the celestial beings in attendance at this council for the whole meaning of this vision. The heavenly being interprets the vision for Daniel, but Daniel ends the chapter feeling very troubled in spirit and, apart from writing it down in Aramaic, keeps the vision to himself.

In the third year of Belshazzar (551 BC), Daniel has another vision (Dan 8). In this vision, which he records in Hebrew and not Aramaic, he sees only two beasts that correspond with two empires: a ram with two horns (Medo-Persia) and a goat that develops four horns (the Macedonian Empire that Alexander the Great starts but leaves subsequently to four of his military subordinates). In this vision, the goat crushes the ram and sprouts the four horns. Alexander died soon after he conquered the vast Persian Empire, and it devolved to four of his generals to rule the rump empire. The generals ruled from different parts: Antipater and later Cassander ruled in Greece and Macedon, Lysimachus in Thrace and large swaths of Asia Minor, Seleucus I Nicator in Mesopotamia and Persia, and Ptolemy I Soter in Egypt and Palestine.

DANIEL'S FIFTH APPEAL: MORE INFORMATION

The focus on Persia and Greece suggests that these two empires (depicted by the vision of the ram and the goat) will have more immediate consequences for the Jewish people soon, leading up to the second century BC. The Persian Empire under Cyrus the Great would allow the release of the Jews back to their homeland in Judea beginning in 538 BC. The Greek Empire will eventually threaten the Jewish people and their religion like no empire before it. If need be, please refer to table 6 in chapter 4 for a depiction of the various empires and their corresponding animals in the different visions.

Daniel seeks to understand the vision. He hears what sounds like a man's voice call out for another celestial being, Gabriel, to explain the vision to Daniel. Gabriel approaches Daniel and explains that these two empires are the Persian and the Greek. He tells Daniel that an evil king will arise at the latter end of the Greek Kingdom. He will be a king of bold face, causing great destruction, and will destroy mighty men and the saints. This wicked king was Antiochus IV Epiphanes (175–64 BC). Epiphanes means "God Manifest," a testimony to his overweening pride in himself. We'll see in the vision of Dan 11 what Antiochus will do, both prophetically and historically.

Gabriel then tells Daniel to seal up the vision—this is perhaps why Daniel records it in Hebrew. The vision is for Daniel's people alone, not the gentile nations in general. This vision leaves Daniel exhausted and ill for several days, and he declares it is beyond his understanding.

Skeptics of the book of Daniel mistakenly conflate the little horn of Dan 8 (Antiochus IV Epiphanes) with the little horn of Dan 7. Note that the little horn of Dan 7 arises during the fourth empire (Rome), not the third (Greek) of Daniel's four empires. The little horn of Antiochus IV Epiphanes arises during the third empire, the Greek/Macedonian, in Dan 8. Conservative scholars believe the little horn of the fourth empire will be the antichrist at the end of history.

As recorded in Dan 9, in about 539 BC, Daniel successfully appealed to the God of heaven for repentance and restoration of the Jewish people. After his prayers during the first year of Darius the Mede, Gabriel returns to Daniel again. Gabriel gives Daniel a prophecy about a coming "Anointed One" who will be put to death and will have nothing. Daniel receives a remarkably accurate prophecy of the coming of Jesus, the Messiah, who will be slain.[1] Gabriel tells Daniel that seventy heptads of years (490 years) are

---

1. See Archer, *Encyclopedia*, 35–36.

decreed for his people "to finish transgression, to put an end to sin, to atone for wickedness, to bring in everlasting righteousness, to seal up the vision and prophecy and to anoint the most holy" (Dan 9:24). Gabriel also tells Daniel that after the killing of the Anointed One, the people of the ruler will come and destroy both the temple and the city of Jerusalem (Titus's conquest of Judah in AD 70). Then wars and desolations will continue until another wicked ruler will arise, who, like Antiochus IV Epiphanes before him, will put an end to sacrifice until he will be killed. This evil ruler will be the little horn of Dan 7 during the final days of the fourth great empire. For this reason and others, the end of the empire is yet future for us.

Many Jewish sects read Daniel's prophecy and anticipated the messiah sometime around the birth, ministry, and death of Jesus, plus or minus a few years, or maybe decades. Despite some exceptions to this generalization, at least three Jewish sects expected the messiah at this time. These sects included the Essenes, the Pharisees, and the Zealots.[2] Because the Samaritans only used the "Samaritan Bible" (the five books of Moses) and not the Jewish prophets, they had less political views of the coming messiah. They were more open to Jesus as the nonpolitical Messiah. The apostle John records this in the story of the Samaritan woman at the well (John 4:1–42).

On the other hand, the Jews had more than simply the books of Moses, including all the major and minor prophets and the wisdom literature or Hagiographa. These works depicted the coming messiah in multiple ways, including as a conquering king. Most Jewish sects interpreted the coming messiah in strongly political terms. The Zealot revolt in AD 66, which led to the Roman conquest of Jerusalem and the destruction of the temple, was full of delayed messianic expectations.[3] Only after the messiah did not come according to these Jewish expectations did some sects adopt a non-messianic interpretation of Daniel's remarkable prophecy in chapter 9.[4]

Daniel 10–12, which occurs two years later in 537 BC, describes how Daniel had another revelation, his final one. He saw a coming great war (or wars, to be more precise). The revelation was so traumatic that he prayed and mourned for three weeks, going without meat, wine, or anointments. During that time, another celestial being approaches Daniel to provide him with an understanding of the vision. The celestial being comes as "a man dressed in linen" (10:5) and appears to Daniel with a visage that defies description. His

2. Beckwith, "Daniel 9," 521.
3. Beckwith, "Daniel 9," 532.
4. Beckwith, "Daniel 9," 522, 536.

DANIEL'S FIFTH APPEAL: MORE INFORMATION

appearance causes so great a terror that Daniel's friends flee from it to hide while Daniel faints with helplessness and pallor. The man in linen is a stock description of a celestial being.[5] Some commentators believe this being may have been Gabriel from Daniel's previous visions, but the text doesn't say so.[6] In fact, Daniel was visited by another unnamed celestial being in Dan 7. Neither the first celestial being nor Gabriel produces such dread in Daniel. The man in linen has to revive Daniel twice while encouraging him several times not to be afraid, stating that Daniel was highly esteemed. He did this so that Daniel could endure what he would see and understand its meaning. The vision and interaction with the man in linen is a single revelation in Dan 10–12. This single vision makes it the longest and fullest description of what will happen to his people. For this reason, it is recorded in Hebrew and not Aramaic.

Daniel 11 reveals events leading up to the persecution of the Jews and then shifts abruptly to a future time at the end of history.[7] Daniel 11:1–4 prophesies the end of the Persian Empire leading up to the conquest of Persia and the death of Alexander the Great. Daniel 11:5–20 depicts the wars between two of the four empires from the remains of the Greek Empire of Alexander—focusing on two, the Ptolemaic and Seleucid Empires up to 168 BC, surrounding Judah. The Ptolemaic Empire is based in Egypt and is called "the king of the South," whereas the Seleucid Empire is based in Syria and Babylon and is called "the king of the North." Daniel 11 depicts the wars between the Seleucid kings and the Ptolemaic kings as the (singular) king of the North versus the (singular) king of the South, which alternately wage war against each other for supremacy in the region for nearly 150 years.

Daniel 11:21–35 then depicts the persecution of Judah and Jewish religious practices by the little horn of Dan 8, Antiochus IV Epiphanes. This persecution was brutal and the biggest threat to Judaism in its history up to that point. According to scholars, Antiochus IV sought to hellenize the Jews completely, to convert them to the Greek language, culture, and religious practices; and to abolish Judaism; he sacrificed pigs on the altar in the temple (profaning the temple and fortress) and outlawed reading from the Torah. He also killed thousands of Jews who revolted against his regime. Antiochus's persecution was an aberration for most ancient rulers, especially the Seleucids, who were more willing to tolerate and encourage

---

5. Heiser, *Unseen Realm*, 119.
6. John J. Collins and Adela Yarbro Collins, *Daniel*, 373.
7. Archer, *Encyclopedia*, 292.

local religious practices, leading some scholars to consider this the beginning of the history of religious persecution.[8]

As mentioned earlier, Antiochus IV gave himself the designation "Epiphanes" or "God manifest." In a play on words, some of his contemporary critics nicknamed him Antiochus Epimanes (the insane or paranoid one).[9] He developed overweening pride to the point of having the following enscription of himself on the coins of his day: Antiochus, God made Manifest, Bearer of Victory.[10] Though Antiochus IV was brutal, he was merely a *type*, a model of what the final wicked king would resemble. In biblical literature, a *type* is an unspoken prophecy, unlike the verbal prophecy we see throughout Scripture. A type of prophecy isn't understood or revealed until after the fact.[11] This type portrays what will come next toward the end of human history with the final wicked ruler in the final gentile kingdom.

The context of the vision shifts subtly in Dan 11:36 and dramatically by v. 40. The king of the North starts doing things that are both unexpected and radically different from that which is known about Antiochus IV Epiphanes. The critical marker is v. 40, where the timestamp is "at the time of the end the king of the South will engage him in battle." This king will be like, but unlike, Antiochus IV. This king will be the "little horn" of Daniel, chapter 7, a horn that will rise in the last days of a Rome yet future. We know this because this wicked ruler will die somewhere in Israel between the sea and the holy mountain, as found in Dan 11:45; we also know this wicked ruler isn't Antiochus because Antiochus died in Persia in 164 BC. This king will not honor the god of his fathers but honor a god of fortresses, a foreign god—something Antiochus did not do. Conservative scholars call this wicked king at the end of the age the antichrist. Table 9 below depicts the differences.

Table 9: Two Little Horns of Daniel	
Antiochus IV Epiphanes	Wicked ruler (antichrist)
3rd empire (Macedonian/Greek)	4th empire (Roman)
Dan 8:9–12, 23–25; 11:21–31	Dan 7:8, 11, 21–26, 11:36–45
Dies outside of Holy Land (Dan 8:25)	Dies in Holy Land (Dan 11:45)
Worships god of his fathers	Doesn't worship god of his fathers (Dan 11:37)

8. Weitzman, "Plotting," 219.
9. Barry, "Antiochus IV," 126.
10. John J. Collins and Adela Yarbro Collins, *Daniel*, 386.
11. Heiser, *Unseen Realm*, 336.

DANIEL'S FIFTH APPEAL: MORE INFORMATION

In Dan 12, the vision continues with the rise of Michael, the great prince of Israel. Michael was featured earlier in this vision, where he comes to help the man in linen. In Dan 10:13, the man in linen comes to provide an understanding of the vision, but Michael has to help him deliver the prophecy. In one of only two passages in the Bible, we see the realm of international politics; the only other depiction of international politics is found in the table of nations in Gen 10.[12] However, this version of international politics depicts the spiritual realm, the cosmic battles between various celestial beings. The prince of Persia resists the man in linen for three weeks but can only delay him for so long once Michael comes to help him. Later, the man in linen will return to Persia to fight the prince of Persia until the prince of Greece comes. At the end of Dan 10, the man in linen tells Daniel that he stood up to help and strengthen Darius the Mede for his rule over Babylon. This revelation tells us that there's more to international conflict than merely human kingdoms competing for power. It tells us that certain celestial beings are princes over nations and that even they may engage in war and conquest against one another along with their human hosts. Many early Christians believed and current Christians believe such princes were charged with ruling the nations, per Deut 32:8, after the Tower of Babel incident. God dispersed humans throughout the earth (Gen 11) to the control of other celestial beings; in Gen 12, God then started over with a new, dedicated people, Israel.[13]

Michael will arise to help Daniel's people at the end of the age. Then there will be a time of trouble that history has never seen, which seems unimaginable. Wars and the ravages of wars have occurred throughout human history, such that, to any individual involved, it would seem like the world was coming to an end. This coming era must be more extraordinary, more distressing, and more horrific than the conquest of the three previous empires of Daniel's visions and the subsequent conquests of Rome—at least for God's holy people. Then, there will be a resurrection of people. The finale to this vision will be Daniel's final appeal, the only appeal he makes that will be declined.

In this chapter, I've used the term "celestial beings." The reason for that is simple. In the Old Testament, a greater variety of terms were employed to understand what would constitute the cosmic realm of the supernatural. The New Testament pattern simplifies the language to angels. But angels in

---

12. Scolnic, "Ptolemaic?," 157–84.
13. Jerome, *Commentary on Daniel*, 114. See also Heiser, *Unseen Realm*, 110–15.

the Old Testament were merely "messengers," whereas various other beings rank above mere messengers. Some celestial beings rule over the nations (Deut 32:8–9). Such beings are called "princes," as in Dan 10. Michael is labeled a chief prince in the Greek version of Dan 11–12. There are also the "watchers," a select group of celestial beings that help decide and deliver God's decrees, as seen in Dan 4:13 and 17. There are "sons of God" present at creation (Job 38:6). There are also those celestial beings who attend God's divine council, as in Dan 7. They are also in the heavenly council in Job 1–2, the setting behind Job's suffering. Then there are a few named beings, particularly Gabriel and a stronger being, the chief prince Michael. Others Daniel encountered remain unnamed.

Though the New Testament pattern simplifies the language, the authors were acutely aware of a wider variety of celestial beings than mere messengers. Paul uses a variety of terms to convey the range of celestial beings he has in mind throughout his letters. In Eph 6:12, he tells us that "our struggle is not against flesh and blood, but against the rulers, against the authorities, against the powers of this dark world and the spiritual forces of evil in the heavenly realms." As Michael Heiser points out, Paul interchanges the terms he uses throughout his letters, including principalities (*arche*), powers/authorities (*exousia*), powers (*dynamis*), dominions/lords (*kyrios*), and thrones (*thronos*). As Heiser points out, "These terms have something in common—they were used in both the New Testament and other Greek literature for geographical domain rulership. This is the cosmic spiritual dominion concept of Deut 32:8–9."[14]

There is a cosmic spiritual geography that informed Daniel's world. More than most authors of prophecies of the Old Testament, Daniel understood the spiritual dimension and interacted with some of these beings. Some of these beings rule over the domains of our planet, likely part of the deeper reason behind the wars of conquest, coups, civil wars, and other conflicts we observe in human history. These beings that rule over domains of the earth continue to resist the great reversal that began when Jesus inaugurated the kingdom of heaven, died, and was resurrected. It is a reversal that will culminate at the end of human history.

---

14. Heiser, *Unseen Realm*, 121.

DANIEL'S FIFTH APPEAL: MORE INFORMATION

THE APPEAL

> But you, Daniel, close up and seal the words of the scroll until the time of the end. Many will go here and there to increase knowledge. Then I, Daniel, looked, and there before me stood two others, one on this bank of the river and one on the opposite bank. One of them said to the man clothed in linen, who was above the waters of the river, "How long will it be before these astonishing things are fulfilled?"
>
> The man clothed in linen, who was above the waters of the river, lifted his right hand and his left hand toward heaven, and I heard him swear by him who lives forever, saying, "It will be for a time, times and half a time. When the power of the holy people has been finally broken, all these things will be completed."
>
> I heard, but I did not understand. So I asked, "My lord, what will the outcomes of this be?"
>
> He replied, "Go your way, Daniel, because the words are rolled up and sealed until the time of the end. Many will be purified, made spotless and refined, but the wicked will continue to be wicked. None of the wicked will understand, but those who are wise will understand." (Dan 12:4–10)

Daniel consistently prepares for what God and his celestial representatives bring him. We saw in Dan 1 that Daniel and his three friends set themselves apart from the rest of the captives by appealing for a unique diet of vegetables and water. While not entirely required by the Mosaic law, this diet helped Daniel and his friends respectfully decline the perquisites of power and avoid cultural and religious absorption into Babylonian practices. He remained obedient to Babylonian governmental leaders even as he remained set apart from the "elite" of Babylon. In his obedience to human authorities, Daniel was obedient to God. The reason for his obedience is that God gave Jeremiah a prophecy that those taken captive to Babylon were to seek the prosperity of Babylon. In his letter to the exiles, Jeremiah reveals that God will honor those who honor Babylon (Jer 29:7).

Daniel faithfully exercises his gifts. In the first chapter, Daniel and his friends are gifted with knowledge and understanding after Daniel's appeal for a restrictive diet. God honors the four of them with the ability to learn and understand the literature and knowledge of the Babylonian graduate school of administration. These four also *worked extremely hard* at their learning. However, in addition to knowledge and understanding, Daniel was explicitly gifted with the ability to understand visions and dreams of all kinds. And those gifts would presently be exercised.

Soon, probably in his second year of training, Daniel's gifts will be tested. Daniel must seek his friends' prayers to see Nebuchadnezzar's dream and understand its meaning. Giftedness and prayer, however, are insufficient by themselves. We see in Dan 2 that Daniel had to bravely trust in God to make his appeal to both the king and to God—to the king for more time and to God for the vision and its understanding. Likewise, in Dan 1, he bravely stepped out in faith when he appealed to the chief of the eunuchs to be allowed to have a separate diet, knowing that defying the king's edicts could end with his death and the death of his friends. In Dan 5, he bravely declines Belshazzar's offer to be promoted to the third position in the kingdom and tells the king what the handwriting on the wall says and what it means. In Dan 6, he bravely continues his public pattern of prayer toward Jerusalem three times a day, knowing that court officials have laid a trap for him. Daniel practiced brave loyalty to God in difficult human conditions while exercising his gifts. And this preparation makes him a fit vessel to receive the subsequent revelations of Dan 7–12.

As we have seen, Daniel was given multiple opportunities to exercise his gifts for receiving and understanding revelations. Daniel was given both Nebuchadnezzar's dream and its understanding (Dan 2). Nearly fifty years later, Daniel received his revelation of history down to the end of time (Dan 7); he appeals for some clarification on significant parts of it. In particular, he was curious about the little horn that would cause so much damage during the last human kingdom. He also received a more detailed revelation of the two empires that would significantly affect his fellow Jews through the second century BC (Dan 8), including another little horn (Antiochus IV Epiphanes) that would seriously threaten Judaism. He subsequently received a unique revelation of the coming Anointed One, who would be cut off (Dan 9). Finally, he received a very long and detailed prophecy down through the end of human history, leading to the establishment of the kingdom of God (Dan 10–12). During these revelations, Daniel would meet several celestial beings, at least one of whom would cause him to faint and require being physically revived more than once to withstand the glory of his presence and endure the confounding vision and its understanding.

Daniel's appeal here in Dan 12 reflects a consistent pattern. Daniel remained very respectful to human authorities, celestial beings, and God. He respected human authorities in Dan 1, 2, 4, and 6. He remained respectful

DANIEL'S FIFTH APPEAL: MORE INFORMATION

of celestial beings as well. In Dan 7, he approached one of the heavenly beings in the presence of the divine council to ask him what the true meaning of the four beasts was and, later, specifically, the meaning of the boastful fourth beast, or the little horn of the fourth empire. In Dan 8, while trying to understand the vision, he was approached by Gabriel and given the understanding of the vision. In Dan 9, he respectfully prays to God for his own and Judah's repentance and restoration from captivity. And finally, in Dan 12:8 he says to the man in linen, "My lord, what will the outcome of these things be?"

Daniel's appeal is appealing for another reason as well. As with human authority, so with divine, Daniel seeks to understand certain things. In Dan 2, Daniel requests to know the urgency of the king's decree, not questioning whether the king had the right or the authority to have all the wise men slain. In Dan 4, despite the alarming nature of Nebuchadnezzar's dream of the tree, Daniel seeks to reassure the king. He also bravely encourages the king that his dream portends a potential threat to his rule and advises him to renounce his sins so that their consequences don't fall on him. How many political advisors in history would have the courage to do that? In all cases where celestial beings give Daniel almost incomprehensible visions and dreams, he works hard to gain understanding or asks for further information. After wrestling with both the presence of the man in linen and the nature of the revelation and after the celestial being's prompting, Daniel asks, "My lord, what will the outcome of all this be?" (Dan 12:8). The pattern continues here with his final appeal.

Daniel politely and respectfully appeals to everyone in authority. He established the pattern early in his youth and maintained it consistently throughout his career, even when put in a trap by his fellow administrators in Dan 6. At least to the king, he remains polite and respectful. He doesn't intervene on behalf of the conspirators when King Darius has them killed. As with human authority, so with divine authority, Daniel remains respectful and skillful in his appeals for further information or clarification of what dreams and visions mean. However, despite this consistency, the man in linen declines Daniel's appeal in Dan 12:8. Perhaps it is simply because the man in linen had already told Daniel in v. 4 to "close up and seal the words of the scroll until the time of the end." Daniel doesn't ask a second time. However, there may be more to the story than this.

We can argue for the best explanation here by examining several reasons, and they may be complementary and mutually reinforcing. First, the most straightforward answer may be that the celestial being had already told Daniel to close up and seal the scroll's words until the end. The man in linen tells Daniel to go his way until the end, where he will rest and rise to receive an inheritance. Second, a more profound explanation may also include what we find in 1 Pet 1:12, where the apostle tells us about the prophets: "It was revealed to them that they were not serving themselves but you, when they spoke of the things that have now been told you by those who have preached the gospel to you by the Holy Spirit sent from heaven. Even angels long to look into these things." That is to say, the information given to Daniel wasn't for his knowledge alone but for future generations that will come after him. Indeed, the celestial being tells Daniel in Dan 12:10 that "many will be purified, made spotless and refined, but the wicked will continue to be wicked. None of the wicked will understand, but those who are wise will understand." Understanding will come to those who choose, like Daniel, to remain dedicated to God's kingdom purposes, and it will come when understanding the final prophecy will be necessary to understand. And, like so many of those who left Jesus after he gave them parables they could not understand, and who did not feel obliged to dig further for understanding, the prophecies given here will not help those who don't seriously commit to God's kingdom purposes in time.

A still deeper reason may lurk underneath both explanations given above. And this explanation may deepen our appreciation for the ambiguity we sometimes see in prophecies, especially revelations about the future. However, to explain this, we may need to refer again to the work of the recently deceased scholar of the Bible, Michael Heiser.[15]

In his book, *The Unseen Realm*, Heiser explains why the New Testament disciples could not understand why Jesus had to die. Heiser uses the metaphor of the messianic mosaic. He explains that no single prophecy about the messiah gave exact details about what would happen to him because God didn't want anyone to know the precise details until it was necessary. In other words, the mosaic of what Jesus had to do wouldn't become apparent until after the fact. The apostle Paul makes it clear why in 1 Cor 2:6–8: "We do, however, speak a message of wisdom among the mature, but not the wisdom of this age or of the *rulers of this age*, who are coming to nothing. No, we declare God's wisdom, a mystery that has been hidden and that God destined for our glory before time began. None of the *rulers of this*

---

15. Heiser, *Unseen Realm*, 240–48.

age understood it, for if they had, they would not have crucified the Lord of Glory" (emphasis added).

Heiser expands on Paul's point that, had God's celestial enemies who ruled over gentile nations known how Jesus would triumph over them, they would not have crucified him.[16] Angels and other heavenly beings longed to look into what would happen and how it would happen. Jesus triumphed over these enemy celestial beings through God's strategy of not coming as a conquering hero (at first) but as a humble servant. God duped the enemy beings into falling into his trap. This is partly why Jesus didn't want human authorities to know his mission either until the time was ripe.

Not only did the celestial beings fail to understand how Jesus would accomplish God's plan, but humans failed to understand as well. In particular, the disciples of Jesus could not understand how Jesus would need to go to the cross to accomplish God's redemptive purposes. Peter failed to understand Jesus' purpose when he opposed Jesus saying he had to go to Jerusalem to suffer and die, for which Jesus rebukes him (Matt 16:23). Luke further tells the story about the disciples who unknowingly meet Jesus after his resurrection on the road to Emmaus in Luke 2:27 and 30–32: "And beginning with Moses and all the Prophets, he explained to them what was said in all the Scriptures concerning himself. When he was at the table with them, he took bread, gave thanks, broke it and began to give it to them. Then their eyes were opened and they recognized him, and he disappeared from their sight. They asked each other, 'Were not our hearts burning within us while he talked with us on the road and opened the Scriptures to us?'" A little later, Jesus appears to the disciples again in Luke 24:44–45: "He said to them, 'This is what I told you while I was still with you: Everything must be fulfilled that is written about me in the Law of Moses, the Prophets and the Psalms.' Then he opened their minds so they could understand the Scriptures."

While I've always wondered what it would have been like to be present when Jesus explained all the prophecies concerning him, I never noticed before that Jesus still had to open people's minds to the truth about him supernaturally. Perhaps that's also the key to the man in linen's answer to Daniel.

The most profound reason for declining Daniel's final appeal may be that God doesn't want enemy celestial beings to know the whole story about the end times. The prophetic or apocalyptic mosaic doesn't reveal how or

---

16. Heiser, *Unseen Realm*, 241–42.

when the final ruler will arise or fall. Along with Daniel, we are given a grand outline leading up to the end of history as we know it but not specific details, just as the prophets foretold about the coming messiah before Jesus was born. We do not, however, have actionable intelligence as to when, where, and exactly how the final beast will rise along with the final wicked ruler. This may be so that enemy celestial beings will be tricked into playing into God's preordained trap for them before establishing his kingdom on earth. Nor, according to the man in linen, do we have a "need to know."[17] In the intelligence business, having a top-secret clearance is insufficient. We must also have a need to know before accessing specific intelligence to be "read in" to this compartmented information. Many of the prophets of old were in the same boat, not knowing how it would all tie together. They didn't have a "need to know."

And so it is with revelation or apocalypses. We can see God's sovereign purposes in history, including the general outline of how things will end. But we are not "read in" to how God will accomplish his purposes. Nor, according to the man in linen, does Daniel or do we "need to know." It will be sufficient to God's purposes that we remain faithful to that which we understand of God's kingdom rule and directions and remain willing to be purified and made righteous, while the wicked will remain wicked. However, there seems to be a promise to those who will live during those awful days. The words on the scrolls are closed and sealed up "until the time of the end" in Dan 12:9. In Dan 12:4, the man in linen tells Daniel that "many will go here and there to increase knowledge." In other words, those who remain faithful to God will likely search the Scriptures for clues while having their minds supernaturally opened when they need that information to act. But God will not "read in" his celestial enemies about how that will happen.

Throughout his life, Daniel remained committed to God's kingdom purposes for his day. Despite all that he went through for nearly eighty years, he remained laser focused on God's sovereign rule and direction for himself and his fellow Jews. And those purposes never veered from the Jewish great commission as depicted in Isa 49:6: "It is too small a thing for you to be my servant, to restore the tribes of Jacob and bring back those of Israel I have kept. I will also make you a light for the Gentiles, that my salvation may reach to the ends of the earth." Daniel evinces this passage throughout his life. Everyone knew he believed in the God of heaven, who

---

17. Best, "Intelligence," 1.

was superior to the pagan gods of the empires he served. He lived as a light for the gentile nations. His prayer of repentance and restoration helped bring the preserved ones of Israel back to their homeland in Judah. Daniel models how we may commit to God's kingdom purposes for our day by remaining faithful to his great commission for our time. We may follow Matt 28:19 by making disciples when and where God directs us as we prepare for those opportunities.

We do have a promise, though. Jesus told his disciples about the signs of the end of the age. In other words, it is the time when the fourth kingdom will be eventually overthrown and the final, heavenly kingdom of God will be established. In Matt 24:14, he says, "And this gospel of the kingdom will be preached in the whole world as a testimony to all nations, and then the end will come." As Daniel, in his day, actively participated in God's direction for his life and the life of God's kingdom purposes, we too are invited to join in God's direction for our life and his kingdom purposes in our day. As to how, when, and where the establishment of the heavenly kingdom of God will occur, we will have to be content, like Daniel, not knowing when that may occur. However, like Daniel, we may remain confident that God will direct history toward that end in good timing. As Daniel did, may we remain faithful in our calling to his kingdom purposes today.

9

Assessing the Reliability of the Book of Daniel

Analysis of Competing Hypotheses

WE ARE NOW AT a place where we assess the reliability of the book of Daniel.[1] Scholars today hold to one of two main hypotheses about the book. Either a single author in the late sixth century BC wrote the book, or it was written during the second century BC (ca. 170 BC) by an anonymous Jew; the purpose of the book, according to these latter scholars, was to encourage the Jews during the reign of Antiochus IV Epiphanes (ca. 174–65 BC), who persecuted the Jews, especially for their faith. Judaism has traditionally confirmed the former thesis since before the time of Christ; and orthodox Christianity has done so since its inception. The latter took hold after the Enlightenment in the West.

Traditional scholars hold that the book of Daniel was written during the late Babylonian and early Persian imperial domination of Mesopotamia and the Middle East. Daniel reports that he was taken hostage by the conquering Babylonians sometime around 605 BC and served them through the end of the Babylonian period (605–539 BC) and at least for a year or two into the Persian Empire. The book of Daniel, in this view, was not written to encourage the Jews during a period of persecution but was written as a genuine account of the court activities of these two empires and as a series of apocalypses (revelations) of future history leading up to the destruction of the temple in AD 70 and beyond. These traditional

1. See appendix A.

scholars argue that the book of Daniel was written by a single author at the end of his long tenure as an administrator for these two empires, likely around 538 BC.

Many recent scholars hold to the second century hypothesis for various reasons. Most, though not all, argue that some anonymous Jew wrote the book, or significant parts of it, during the reign of Antiochus IV Epiphanes to encourage the Jews when their faith was under assault from that diabolical king. For this reason, this approach to the book of Daniel is called the late-date—or Maccabean—hypothesis because it would have been penned during the Maccabean revolt against the Seleucid Empire in 167–64 BC. Most of these scholars argue that the apocalypses (revelations) were *vaticinium ex eventu* (after the fact), which means that Daniel's prophetic accuracy up to the time of Antiochus IV could only be explained if the anonymous author wrote it during the time of that particular king's reign. In other words, the book of Daniel was not prophetic. And, so, his prophecies of the future are false, too.

Scholars from both sides of the debate use internal and external evidence to support their positions. Internal evidence is generally taken from the book itself or from other parts of the Bible. External evidence comes from history, archeology, or written records. To assess these two hypotheses, we will test the arguments and evidence used by both sides to determine which hypothesis may be more reliable or more coherent. Separately, we will also evaluate some unstated assumptions both sides hold. As mentioned earlier, the facts do not always speak for themselves. Assumptions frequently direct our inquiry and guide us when we marshal evidence, allowing us to connect the dots when many things may be unclear. Such assumptions may cause us to ignore, downplay, or distort disconfirming evidence. This is true for all of us, so we will assess the evidence and arguments alone using the intelligence analysis technique an Analysis of Competing Hypotheses (ACH). We will also evaluate the unstated assumptions that underlie each hypothesis using a method called a Key Assumptions Check.[2]

It becomes vitally important to test the available evidence for the two hypotheses on their terms, apart from their underlying assumptions. That is to say, we will assess the various lines of evidence against the two hypotheses first before evaluating the assumptions. Using ACH, we aim to assess and determine which hypothesis has the most confirming evidence and which has the least disconfirming evidence. This also helps us avoid the

---

2. Both of these techniques may be found in Heuer and Pherson, *Structured Techniques*.

"hypothesis confirming bias" we mentioned earlier. The hypothesis with the least disconfirming evidence is likely the best explanation for the authorship of the book of Daniel.

Appendix A contains table 12, "Analysis of Competing Hypotheses (ACH)." It also includes a list of references for the items of evidence and a scoring system for weighing how a line of evidence or argument confirms or disconfirms each hypothesis or is nondiagnostic for assessing a hypothesis' relative strengths or weaknesses. Table 13, "Key Assumptions Check," is in appendix B.

The results of the ACH seem clear after evaluating the two hypotheses against the available evidence and arguments. The hypothesis (H_1) that the author of the book was a single person situated in the late sixth century BC has the least *disconfirming* (-5) evidence and the most *confirming* (36) evidence for it. Given this, I assess that it is "almost certainly" (95–99 percent) true that a single author, probably Daniel, wrote the book sometime in the late sixth century BC. The hypothesis (H_2) that an anonymous Jew wrote the book of Daniel during the second century BC has the most *disconfirming* (36) and least *confirming* (5) arguments and evidence in its favor. Consequently, I assess that there is "almost no chance" (1–5 percent) that it is accurate or the best explanation of the book's authorship. (See table 11 below for "Probabilities Within a Fuzzy System"). Arguing for the best explanation leads a dispassionate reader to accept the authorship of the book of Daniel.

Four main sub-hypotheses support this assessment:

1. There is overwhelming evidence that Daniel was recognized, by name, as the book's author by (a) a contemporary in Babylon, (b) subsequent Jewish scholars, (c) several New Testament authors, (d) a non-Christian, Jewish Roman historian, and (e) the early church fathers. Jesus acknowledged Daniel—again, by name—as the book's author.

2. The book of Daniel exhibits coherence and a point of view that makes it likely the work of a single author from the late sixth century BC.

3. The author's use of various languages, including Hebrew, Aramaic, Persian, and Greek, points to a single author in the late sixth century BC.

4. The author's knowledge of critical people, religion, and details of court life in Babylon would unlikely have been known with such detail after the fifth century BC—at least until modern archeology dating from the nineteenth century AD was available.

We will examine these sub-hypotheses and then assess H_2, the late-date authorship.

Hypothesis 1: The book of Daniel was written in the late sixth century by a single author, likely by the name of Daniel. Four sub-hypotheses support this.

Sub-hypothesis #1: There is overwhelming evidence that Daniel was recognized, by name, as the book's author by (a) a contemporary in Babylon, (b) subsequent Jewish scholars, (c) several New Testament authors, (d) a non-Christian, Jewish Roman historian, and (e) the early church fathers. Jesus acknowledged Daniel—again, by name—as the book's author.

This sub-hypothesis focuses on how early Jews and Christians—Jesus included—viewed the book's authorship. First, a near contemporary of Daniel, the prophet Ezekiel, refers to him twice in his book, probably published about thirty years after Daniel established his career and reputation in the court of Babylon. Human sources of information are considered more reliable when proven trustworthy over time. Ezekiel had this in spades. He was likely taken in the second wave of exiles around 597 BC, about 7–8 years after Daniel, who was taken in the first wave, ca. 605 BC, and would have been intimately familiar with Daniel's growing reputation. Daniel had plenty of time to establish his bona fides before Ezekiel began his ministry (ca. 593 BC). In Ezek 14:14–20, Daniel is praised for his righteousness; in Ezek 28:3, he is praised for his wisdom and his ability to solve "mysteries"—that is, Ezekiel records the two things that stand out about Daniel's career as recorded in the book of Daniel.

Some second century advocates argue that Ezekiel's Daniel refers to someone other than the traditional subject of the book of Daniel. In Ezek 14:14 and 20, Noah, Job, and Daniel are included as among the three most righteous men who lived. These critics argue that since Noah and Job were not Jewish (or Israelite), the Daniel listed with them must be someone else. Instead, they point to a certain Dnil of the Ugaritic myth of Aqhat.[3] The

---

3. In his book *Prophecy*, Callahan dismisses the author as the traditional Daniel in favor of the Ugaritic Dnil without giving much attention to the details of either the myth or the tradition. See Callahan, *Prophecy*, 149. A better discussion, pro and con, can be found by two scholars, Dressler, "Identification," 152–61 and the response in Day, "Daniel of Ugarit," 174–84. For a discussion of these two works, see Bible.org, "Who Is

Daniel in Babylon

Dnil in Ugaritic myth, however, was not characterized by either righteousness or wisdom in the Hebrew sense of the words.[4] Further, the Dnil of Ugaritic myth was a Canaanite Baal worshiper—unlike either Noah or Job, who worshipped the one true God. It is far more likely that the prophet Ezekiel would have referred to the contemporary, exiled Jew, who, like him, had established an outstanding reputation for his wisdom and righteousness among the exilic Jews in Babylon. Contemporary Jews in exile would be far more likely to know of Daniel from his actions in Babylon than from a pagan myth dating at least six centuries earlier. This myth was not recorded or acknowledged by any other book in the Old Testament. Critics also have to ignore Ezek 28:3, where the prophet asks whether anyone is wiser than Daniel who can unveil mysteries, as Daniel did throughout his book. The Dnil of myth did no such thing.

Every part of Daniel's book was preserved in the Dead Sea Scrolls of Qumran. This community existed around 150 BC.[5] It is highly unlikely that the community at Qumran would have regarded the book of Daniel as authentic had it been recently written or portions of it written by an anonymous Jew living near contemporary (167–64 BC) to the reign of Antiochus IV Epiphanes. Indeed, Jewish scholars had a test for the reliability of prophets and prophecy, which had been laid out in Deut 18:22: "If what a prophet proclaims in the name of the LORD does not take place or come true, that is a message the LORD has not spoken. The prophet has spoken presumptuously, so do not be alarmed." As Jewish scholars noted, Daniel's prophetic accuracy until Antiochus Epiphanes was outstanding.[6] While there were other documents at Qumran (e.g., The Manual of Discipline, The War of the Children of Light Against the Children of Darkness), they shared nothing in common with the more ancient book of Daniel. They were, therefore, never included in sacred Scriptures.[7]

The book of Daniel and other Old Testament books are part of the Tanakh in Hebrew. The Tanakh went through a process of canonization—a form of scholarly testing and validation of the reliability of ancient books. The Tanakh has three distinct divisions: the law of Moses (Torah), the Prophets (Nevim), and the writings (Kethuvim) or Hagiographa. Jewish

---

Ezekiel's Daniel?"

4. Edlin, *Daniel*, 29.
5. Haughwot, *Dating Daniel*, 12.
6. Leiman, *Canonization*, 37.
7. Archer, *Survey*, 400.

scholars believe prophecy ceased in the fifth century BC.[8] Some critics question the book of Daniel's authenticity because it is included in the Hagiographa rather than the Prophets. However, in all the canons listed by Josephus, the Septuagint, and the Talmud it is indicated that "in most Jewish circles, the Prophets and Hagiographa were treated alike."[9]

All thirty-nine Old Testament books are the same as the twenty-two or twenty-four books of the Tanakh. All were considered to be both "inspired" by God and "canonical." In the talmudic tradition, "Jews accept canonical book as authoritative for religious practice and doctrine, and whose authority is binding upon the Jewish people for all generations. Furthermore, such books are to be studied and expounded in private and in public." By inspiration, talmudic scholars examined the work to determine whether it was "composed under divine inspiration"[10]—that is to say, whether God spoke the words or whether he gave the words to the prophets. According to Jewish scholarship, Hebrew Scriptures in Jewish and Christian traditions were considered "inspired" and "canonical." Some Jewish literature may be regarded as canonical but uninspired—but not the Tanakh, our Old Testament. For example, the Mishnah (exegetical material, judgments, and rulings on the law by talmudic scholars) is considered canonical but uninspired in Jewish tradition.[11]

Jewish scholars considered the book of Daniel to be both inspired and canonical. By the first century AD, if not before the time of Qumran, talmudic scholars considered all of the books of the Tanakh as canonical and inspired.[12] There remains some uncertainty about when the canonization process may have occurred; more likely, it may have happened in stages, with the law of Moses first, followed by the Prophets second, and the Hagiographa third. A fair reading of Dan 9:2 suggests that the prophetic books were already considered canonical when Daniel wrote his book.

Additionally, the Christians of the early church, including Jesus, the apostles, and the early church fathers, accepted the book of Daniel as inspired and canonical. New Testament authors believed Daniel, from the sixth century BC, was the author of the book of Daniel. They affirmed the canonicity and inspiration of Daniel, and they cite Daniel in several places,

---

8. Leiman, *Canonization*, 128–31.
9. Leiman, *Canonization*, 33.
10. Leiman, *Canonization*, 14–15.
11. Leiman, *Canonization*, 15.
12. Leiman, *Canonization*, 35, 37.

including Heb 11:33–34 and possibly Luke 1:11–20 and 26–28. The book of Daniel was the basis for much of the apostle Paul's "expositions on resurrection and the return of Christ" in 1 Thess 4–5, 2 Thess 2, and 1 Cor 15.[13] The Apostle John incorporated many of Daniel's apocalypses in the book of Revelation. Even more importantly, several sections of the book of Daniel are quoted by Jesus himself, who refers to Daniel as a natural person and a prophet. Jesus' citations include portions of Dan 3 (in Matt 13:42, 50), Dan 7 (Matt 24:30; Mark 13:26, 14:26), Dan 9 (Matt 24:15), and Dan 11 (Mark 13:13). When Jesus refers to the person of Daniel in Matt 24:15, he also uses the Greek preposition *dia*, which emphasizes "personal agency," implying the existence of an actual, natural person.[14]

The New Testament understanding of inspiration is similar to the Jewish understanding. This makes sense as the early converts were Jewish. In 2 Tim 3:16–17, the apostle Paul declares, "All Scripture is God-breathed and useful for teaching, rebuking, correcting and training in righteousness, so that the servant of God may be thoroughly equipped for every good work." God-breathed is a literal translation of the Greek word *theopneustos*, from which we get our term "inspiration." God actively breathed his ideas to and through the writers of the Holy Scriptures without changing their personalities, vocabulary, or idioms. God initiated and provided the coherence of the message, not the human authors. The apostle Peter makes a similar claim in 2 Pet 1:20–21: "Above all, you must understand that no prophecy of Scripture came about by the prophet's own interpretation. For prophecy never had its origin in the human will, but prophets, though human, spoke from God as they were carried along by the Holy Spirit." Human will cannot prompt God's inspiration. Christians applied this maxim along with other criteria to determine the inspiration and canonicity of the Old and New Testament works, and the book of Daniel has always been regarded as among them.

Another person who also believed in the authenticity of the book of Daniel was Josephus. Josephus was a Roman Jew who wrote a history of the Jewish people. He was neither a Christian nor an observant Jew. Relaying the oral tradition of the Jews in the first century AD, Josephus explained that when Alexander the Great came to Jerusalem in 332 BC, Jaddua the high priest showed him—among the other inspired and canonical books of

---

13. Edlin, *Daniel*, 20.
14. Archer, *Survey*, 408.

the Tanakh—the book of Daniel, which predicted the rise of the Greek and Roman Empires.[15]

Early church fathers also accepted the inspiration and canonicity of the book of Daniel. The term canon, from the Greek, means rule or measuring stick. It refers to the standard, rule, or measure for how we are to live. The church fathers that regarded Daniel as authentic include Melito, bishop of Sardis (ca. AD 170); Origen of Alexandria and Caesarea (ca. AD 185–225); Epiphanius, bishop of Salamis in Cyprus (ca. AD 315–403); and Jerome of Bethlehem (ca. AD 347–419), among others.[16] The book's only "early" critic was Porphyry, the third century AD non-Christian Neoplatonist, with a personal axe to grind against Christianity.[17]

Sub-hypothesis #2: The book of Daniel exhibits a coherence and point of view that likely makes it the work of a single author from the late sixth century.

A quick reminder about the structure of the book of Daniel. The first six chapters are considered Babylonian and Persian court narratives. The last six chapters (7–12) are apocalypses or revelations. However, that is only part of the picture, as Dan 2 documents King Nebuchadnezzar's revelation of future kingdoms that only Daniel can understand. Further, although the English translation does not show this, about half of the book is written in Hebrew (chapters 1–2a; 8–12), and the other half is written in Aramaic (chapters 2b–7).

The simple division of the book into Hebrew and Aramaic, or narrative and apocalyptic chapters, belies the author's brilliant and more complex organization. First, the book displays coherence across the Aramaic chapters (2–7) through a chiasm, an inverted structure like an X. The chiasm in Daniel uses five narrative chapters and one apocalyptic chapter. A chiasm is a literary device in which parallel sections appear in an inverted arrangement (see table 10, "Chiasm in Daniel 2–7," below).[18] Chapters 2 and 7 form an outer parallel in which Nebuchadnezzar and Daniel dream about four earthly kingdoms and a fifth eternal kingdom. The core of the

---

15. See Josephus, *Antiquities*, 368; see also Gaebelein, *Prophet Daniel*.
16. Leiman, *Canonization*, 31–50.
17. Jerome (ca. AD 340–420) and others contended with Porphyry's claim early on.
18. Widder, "Heart and Hope," 31.

chiasm is the parallel between chapter 4, in which a proud gentile king (Nebuchadnezzar) is humbled, and chapter 5, where yet another proud gentile king (Belshazzar) is humbled. Chapters 3 and 6 parallel what righteous believers can expect from human rule. In Dan 3, Daniel's friends face death for their faith, and Daniel faces his own death for his faith in Dan 6. The remainder of the book amplifies the horrific persecution the Jews will face under gentile kingdoms, up to and including end times.

Table 10: Chiasm in Daniel 2–7[19]			
A, Nebuchadnezzar dreams of four earthly and a fifth eternal kingdom (Dan 2)			
	B, Daniel's friends face death for their faith (Dan 3)		
		C, Nebuchadnezzar humbled (Dan 4)	
		C^1, Belshazzar humbled (Dan 5)	
	B^1, Daniel faces death for his faith (Dan 6)		
A^1, Daniel dreams of four earthly and a fifth eternal kingdom (Dan 7)			

In addition to Daniel's chiastic structure for chapters 2–7, he crafts chapter 7 (the last of the Aramaic and first of the apocalyptic chapters) as the linchpin between the book's narrative sections (chs. 1–6) and the Hebrew language apocalypses (chs. 8–12). Chapters 1–12 are all primarily set during Daniel's lifetime, but chapters 7–12 provide revelations of the future. Chapters 1–6 focus on God's sovereign rule over gentile empires; chapters 7–12 focus on Daniel's visions of the future rule of gentile empires and the suffering believers can expect until the Messiah sets up an eternal kingdom on earth; chapter 7 belongs to both sections. "It reiterates the succession of ancient Gentile kingdoms, yet it provides more detail about the 'latter days' when the Antichrist will arise."[20]

The court narratives are necessary for a Jewish prophet before the apocalyptic chapters. They establish Daniel's bona fides to a Jewish audience. Recall from the first sub-hypothesis, to be accepted, a prophet has to tell what is reliably true before the people can receive the prophet's claim for future events. Jewish scholars relied on Deut 18:22 for an internal test of prophecy. Daniel's accurate descriptions of the courts of Babylon and Persia established his trustworthiness for his later revelations.

---

19. Adapted from Widder, "Heart and Hope," 31.
20. Tanner, "Literary Structure," 278.

Another essential element of cohesion is the various appeals Daniel makes throughout his career, which display preparation, wisdom, humility, submission, and personal righteousness. These appeals are made to progressively higher authority, both within human governments and beyond them, including an appeal to an archangel, Gabriel, and to God himself. I addressed these appeals earlier in this book—how Daniel prepared—including establishing a solid reputation in his work ethic, the study of prophecy, submission to God in religious rituals, and individual and corporate prayer—and how the appeals wisely left the decisions in the hands of superiors. In summary, though, the five progressive appeals Daniel makes are as follows:

1. Daniel 1:8–10: Daniel appeals to the commander of officials to choose a vegetarian diet to avoid defiling himself.
2. Daniel 2:14–28: Daniel appeals to Arioch, the captain of the king's bodyguards, to seek God's help in revealing Nebuchadnezzar's dreams.
3. Daniel 6:1–24: Daniel makes an appeal without words to King Darius, who was tricked by his sub-officials into framing Daniel for violating a political order.
4. Daniel 9:1–23: Daniel appeals to God for the forgiveness of Israel's sins and is met by an angel, Gabriel, who gives him further information on the future of Israel.
5. Daniel 12:1–9: Daniel appeals to God's representative for further information on the visions and revelations for the end times but is denied.

Sub-hypothesis #3: The author of the book of Daniel wrote the book using ancient Aramaic and Hebrew for distinct purposes and different audiences, borrowing available "loan" words from Greek and Persian where appropriate.

Daniel wrote this book in two different languages. Chapters 1—2:4a and 8–12 were written in Hebrew. In contrast, chapters 2:4b—7:28 were written in ancient Imperial (or Eastern, non-Palestinian) Aramaic.[21] An author writing in Aramaic in the second century would have used a Palestinian dialect of Aramaic. The Aramaic portion of the book has been assessed as older than the Hebrew portion, probably because of Jewish scholars' scribal

---

21. Archer, *Survey*, 397.

transmission of the Hebrew chapters over the years. It is similar to the fifth century BC Elephantine Papyri of a Jewish community in southern Egypt.[22] Only one other book of the Old Testament, Ezra 4:8—6:8 and 7:12–26, from the middle of the fifth century BC, includes a significant portion in Imperial Aramaic and has been accepted as authentic.[23]

Daniel wrote in two different languages with two distinct audiences in mind. Because Aramaic was the *lingua franca* of the day, the messages in those sections were for a wider audience of Jews and gentiles living in Babylon. The Hebrew portion was written with Jewish concerns in mind, such as the future of Judah under gentile kingdoms—concerns of less interest and importance to gentiles themselves.[24] In Dan 12:9, the prophet is told that parts of the text were to be closed and sealed up for a yet future age, which are the sections that give skeptics the most pause.

Daniel also uses foreign "loan" words. The book uses three Greek words for musical instruments and fifteen Persian words for politics and administration.[25] Skeptics of Daniel's authorship claim that Daniel's use of the three Greek words, all for musical instruments, places his writing during the second century BC during the reign of Antiochus IV Epiphanes. They argue this because Palestine had been hellenized from the time of Alexander the Great (ca. 334 BC).[26] The process of Hellenization—the imposition of Greek culture, religion, and language—transformed government and politics, language and culture, and eventually the Jewish religion through the period of the Maccabean revolt.[27]

However, Greek culture and language had passed into the Levant and even to Mesopotamia by the tenth century BC, several hundred years before the book of Daniel was written.[28] Greek words for musical instruments would have easily been available throughout the Near East and the broader Middle East, especially with the large numbers of Greek mercenaries used by different empires in Mesopotamia before the rise of Babylon. More

22. Archer, *Survey*, 397.
23. Archer, *Survey*, 397, 399.
24. Archer, *Survey*, 399.
25. Three Persian words for government and politics are used in the Hebrew portions and fifteen in the Aramaic portions of the book. See Archer, *Survey*, 397.
26. For the harp (*qithros*, from the Greek *kitharis*); for the psaltry (*pesanerin* from the Greek *psateiron*); and for the dulcimor (*sumponeyah* from the Greek *symphonia*). See Archer, *Survey*, 395–96.
27. Schiffman, "Hellenism."
28. Yamauchi, "Daniel and Contacts," 37–47.

importantly, contrary to the critics, if a pseudonymous Jew had authored the work during the second century BC, he would have used far more Greek words, particularly for government and politics. Greek had been widely used in Palestine for more than 160 years before Antiochus IV.

Even more importantly, Daniel uses only Persian loan words for government and politics, which situates the work more neatly during the late sixth century BC, after the fall of Babylon to the Medo-Persian Empire in 539 BC, where Daniel also served in the new government at the time of his writing. It is doubtful that an author during the second century would have used so many Persian load words for government and administration instead of Greek.

Sub-hypothesis #4: The author's knowledge of critical people, religion, and details of court life in Babylon was unlikely to have been known with such detail after the fifth century BC—at least until modern archeology dating from the nineteenth century AD.

Only an author in the late sixth century BC (probably 538 BC) would have known the intimate details of the Babylonian Empire's court life and its critical personnel. Within fifty years of the empire's fall to the Medes and Persians, Babylon's palaces and temples, including the walls depicting its art and its rulers, were destroyed by Xerxes, around 480 BC.[29] Writing in 450 BC, the Greek historian Herodotus, who visited Babylon sometime before his book, does not mention any record of the critical figures of Nebuchadnezzar and Belshazzar. He offers no description of the imperial court. On the other hand, "the author [Daniel] possessed a more accurate knowledge of Neo-Babylonian and early Achaemenid Persian history than any other known historian since the sixth century BC."[30]

Furthermore, it's doubtful a pseudonymous author of the second century would have known or understood the distinct political systems and styles of rule between Babylon and Persia. Such an author could not have known that Nebuchadnezzar could enact and modify Babylonian laws with complete sovereignty (Dan 2:12, 48) while also reporting that Darius was powerless to change the "laws of the Medes and the Persians" (Dan 6:8–9; Esth 1:9, 8:8).[31] Nor would a second century BC pseudonymous author

---

29. Conklin, "Evidences," 5.
30. Waltke, "Textual," 328, cited in Conklin, "Evidences," 9.
31. Conklin, "Evidences," 17.

have known that Nabopolassar, Nebuchadnezzar's father, was of lowly background. The first part, or root, of Nabopolassar, Nabo, means "in my littleness." Archeological inscriptions discovered during the nineteenth century refer to Nabopolassar as "the son of a nobody" and socially "describing himself as 'the insignificant,' 'not visible,' 'the weak' and the 'feeble.'"[32] Dan 4:17 depicts God as "sovereign over the kingdoms on earth and gives them to anyone he wishes and sets them over the lowliest of people."

Only an author of the sixth century BC could have known about King Belshazzar and his place in the royal court or in the royal line of succession. Historians have known that Nabonidus was the last king of the Babylonian Empire. Until discoveries of cuneiform tablets "referring to Belshazzar as 'the son of the king'" were discovered, critics pointed to this as a historical error in Daniel.[33] Belshazzar was appointed as regent in his father's place, while Nabonidus went out to subdue his opponents. Daniel correctly observed in Dan 5:16, however, that Belshazzar only promised him (Daniel) to be promoted to third ruler in the kingdom, as Belshazzar was second to his father. Even after the tablets established Daniel's trustworthiness, some critics still go further, pointing out that Belshazzar was not Nebuchadnezzar's son but Nabonidus's son. However, such criticism fails to acknowledge that the ancients frequently referred to sons as successors in office, which has been observed in Jewish and Egyptian sources contemporary with the time of Daniel.[34]

Hypothesis 2: The book of Daniel was written by an anonymous Jew living during the second century BC.

Proponents of the second century authorship of the book of Daniel share in what is called a modern scholarly consensus. This consensus holds that because Daniel's "prophecies" were accurate up to the time of Antiochus IV Epiphanes, his prophecies were *vaticinium ex eventu* (after the fact). In other words, Daniel's future prophecies of the Persian conquest of Babylon, the Macedonian conquest of Persia, and the internecine warfare between two elements of Alexander the Great's successor kingdoms were written not as prophecy but as history. This holds for all the apocalyptic elements in the book of Daniel, particularly in chapters 7–12.

---

32. McDowell, *Critic's Den*, 12–13.
33. Archer, *Survey*, 391.
34. Archer, *Survey*, 391.

ASSESSING THE RELIABILITY OF THE BOOK OF DANIEL

Such proponents point to the fact that the book of Daniel stops being accurate about what we know of Antiochus IV Epiphanes around Dan 11:36. Several things stand out. Antiochus Epiphanes was, for the Jews, a heinous king; historians have claimed that the history of religious persecution could be said to have begun with him.[35] After his failed second attempt to conquer the king of the South (the Ptolemaic Empire), Antiochus Epiphanes returned home in wrath and plundered the temple in Jerusalem, set up an altar to the pagan god Zeus Olympias, and killed thousands of Jews while outlawing their religious practices. However, the subsequent behavior of this heinous king does not follow what we know of Antiochus Epiphanes. The real Antiochus died in Persia, not Jerusalem (Dan 11:44–45). Antiochus did not abandon the pagan faith of his fathers (Dan 11:37).

Late-date proponents then cast about for an explanation for why the book was written. While various ideas have been proposed, none seem that convincing. The most significant argument is that this anonymous Jew wrote the book of Daniel to encourage Jews during this horrible time—often pointing to Nebuchadnezzar's madness (Dan 4:31–35) in comparison to Antiochus Epiphanes.[36] That said, the author of the book of Daniel, in chapters 2–4, depicts Nebuchadnezzar favorably, something the Jewish contemporaries of Antiochus never did.[37] It also remains unclear how Nebuchadnezzar's restoration in the latter part of Dan 4 (vv. 34–37) would have encouraged the Jewish people if it were meant to refer to Antiochus. Ultimately, Antiochus was overthrown by the Jewish revolt against the Seleucids, leading to the Maccabean period of Jewish history.

Conservative or traditional scholars, on the other hand, argue that Antiochus Epiphanes was a type.[38] As mentioned before, a type is a form of unspoken prophecy that foreshadows what is to come but will only be understood until after the fact. We are familiar with spoken or verbal prophecy, where the prophet tells the reader what can be expected. A type is an unspoken prophecy that foreshadows what will come. Types or typologies are used throughout the Bible. The first man, Adam, foreshadows Jesus Christ, according to the apostle Paul in Rom 5:14. As egregious as Antiochus's behavior toward the Jews and their faith was, this future king, at

---

35. Weitzman, "Plotting," 219.
36. Callahan, *Prophecy*, 164, 177; Haughwot, *Dating Daniel*, 35.
37. Archer, *Survey*, 410, quoting Gustav Hoelscher's *Die Entstehung des Buches Daniel* (1919).
38. Heiser, *Unseen Realm*, 336–37.

the end of time, will be far more wicked. Antiochus Epiphanes foreshadows the final wicked ruler, the antichrist, who will eventually die in Jerusalem. Thus, the type of Antiochus Epiphanes in Dan 11:36—12:13 foreshadows the culminating period in world history before the return of Jesus Christ and inaugurates the final kingdom that will destroy all human kingdoms. Remember, too, that there were two "little horns" in Daniel's prophecies: one that would emerge from the third kingdom (Antiochus IV Epiphanes) and one from the fourth kingdom (the future antichrist).

Daniel also related many prophecies for which the late-date authorship hypothesis cannot account. Several stand out as they relate to events that have occurred in history since the second century BC but before the end times. The first is that in both Dan 2 and 7, Daniel points to the emergence of the fourth empire of Rome. Though Rome had been around for some time and had established a vassal protectorate in Egypt, it only took control over the Levant in 63 BC.[39] Second, as we saw in his fourth appeal, Daniel was given a prophecy of the coming of the messiah, which most Jews believed would occur around the time that Jesus came to do his work. Sometime during his ministry, he would be put to death (Dan 9:26). During his earthly ministry, Jesus believed that the Abomination of Desolation mentioned by Daniel (Dan 9:27, 11:31, 12:11) was still in the future and was not the work of Antiochus. Finally, Daniel (Dan 9:25–27) predicts the destruction of the temple after the messiah was cut off, which eventually occurred in AD 70.[40]

Many of Daniel's other prophecies remain for the future or toward the end times. But, as Deuteronomy requires, Daniel's history and short-term prophecies must first be proven true. Only after that can we trust his long-term, yet-to-be-fulfilled prophecies. However, just as the prophecies of the messiah and his coming were a mosaic and not a linear prediction, the other prophecies are a mosaic. Just as Antiochus represents the antichrist as a type, Daniel's end-times prophecies will not be fully understood until the time is ripe for them to be. The words of Daniel have been preserved, or "sealed up," so that when that understanding is finally necessary, the latent information in the book of Daniel will help the righteous understand what unfolds before their eyes.

---

39. Archer, *Survey*, 407.
40. Haughwot, *Dating Daniel*, 18–19.

Table 11: Probabilities Within a "Fuzzy" System[41]			
Greater than 50 percent	Percentage	Less than 50 percent	Percentage
Almost Certain	95–99%	Unlikely	20–45%
Very Likely	80–95%	Very Unlikely	5–20%
Likely	55–80%%	Almost No Chance	1–5%
Roughly Even Chance	45–55%		

KEY ASSUMPTIONS CHECK (SEE APPENDIX B)

We are at a point where conducting a Key Assumptions Check becomes essential. In table 13, appendix B, we point out that the assumptions of each position cancel each other out. Hypothesis 1 (H_1) assumes that a transcendent God created the entire universe. Therefore, prophecy is not only possible but likely. Hypothesis 2 (H_2) believes that there is no God and that prophecy is impossible, or a variation on it: God may exist, but humans lie, contradicting the assumption of prophecy's truthfulness. It is, therefore, incumbent on us to evaluate the lines of evidence that favor or disfavor each hypothesis (appendix A). Did a single author write the book of Daniel in the late sixth century BC, or did an anonymous Jew write the book in the second century BC?

As we have seen above, there are fewer *disconfirming* lines of evidence (5) and more *confirming* items of evidence (36), favoring H_1—that the book of Daniel was written by a single author in the late sixth century BC. On the other hand, there are far more *disconfirming* items of evidence (36) and far fewer *confirming* lines of evidence (5) for H_2—that an anonymous Jew wrote the book of Daniel in the second century BC. This strongly suggests that the assumptions, not the evidence, drive the second-century-authorship hypothesis. The advocates for this latter view would be well-served by explicitly stating their assumptions and revising their interpretation of the book's authorship accordingly.

Does this support the view with absolute certainty that Daniel wrote the book of Daniel in the sixth century BC? No, it does not. The purpose of using the ACH and the Key Assumptions Check is to test the available evidence and arguments against the competing hypotheses to determine which one may be said to reason to the best hypothesis, a good form of

---

41. Office of the Director of National Intelligence, *Intelligence Directive 203*.

abductive reasoning. The Key Assumptions Check lets us know whether the evidence or our explicit or implicit assumptions drive the analysis. In our case, the results of the ACH and assumptions check strongly suggest that Daniel authored the book in the sixth century.

Just because the book of Daniel is difficult doesn't make it untrue. On the contrary, there is much to commend us to believe it is reliably accurate. I think we can be encouraged by these lines of evidence that support the argument that Daniel authored the book during the sixth century BC and not shy away from our trust in the God of the universe and the words of the Bible. Put simply, the book of Daniel stands the test and may be considered an inspired book of the Bible, which still speaks to us today.

Appendix A: Analysis of Competing Hypotheses

THERE ARE TWO HYPOTHESES under consideration in this analysis. They are:

1. H_1: Daniel was written in the sixth century BC.
2. H_2: Daniel was written in the second century BC.

Table 12 below details the short form of evidence and arguments for each hypothesis.

Table 12: Analysis of Competing Hypotheses (ACH)				
Item	Evidence	Credibility	H:1	H:2
1	*Two Languages*	*Almost Certain*	1	1^1
2	Aramaic purpose	Very Likely	1	-1
3	Hebrew purpose	Very Likely	1	-1
4	Fifth-century Aramaic	Almost Certain	1	-1
5	Imperial style of Aramaic	Very Likely	1	-1
6	*Greek music words*	*Almost Certain*	1	1
7	No Greek for politics	Almost Certain	1	-1
8	Persian loan words for politics	Almost Certain	1	-1
9	Belshazzar, 19th c.	Almost Certain	1	-1
10	Babylon lost to history	Very Likely	1	-1
11	Herodotus and Belshazzar	Very Likely	1	-1
12	Nabopolassar was "lowly"	Very Likely	1	-1
13	Court life of empires	Very Likely	1	-1
14	Succession of empires	Very Likely	1	-1
15	Description of geography	Almost Certain	1	-1

1. Evidence that is nondiagnostic are set in italics, as they confirm both views.

APPENDIX A: ANALYSIS OF COMPETING HYPOTHESES

16	Religion and pantheon	Almost Certain	1	-1
17	Narrative coherence	Almost Certain	1	-1
18	Chiastic structure unity	Almost Certain	1	-1
19	Contemporary citation	Almost Certain	1	-1
20	Qumran citation	Almost Certain	1	-1
21	Sectarian differences	Almost Certain	1	-1
22	Jewish canonicity of Daniel	Almost Certain	1	-1
23	Test of prophecy	Very Likely	1	-1
24	Jesus refers to Daniel	Almost Certain	1	-1
25	Jesus cites Aramaic	Almost Certain	1	-1
26	Paul and John cite Daniel	Almost Certain	1	-1
27	Church fathers canon	Almost Certain	1	-1
28	Josephus and Daniel	Likely	1	-1
29	*Confusion on 11:36–40*	*Very Likely*	*1*	*1*
30	Daniel predicts Roman conquest	Very Likely	1	-1
31	Temple destruction, AD 70	Very Likely	1	-1
32	Nebuchadnezzar and AE II	Almost Certain	1	-1
33	No outside mention of Daniel	Very Likely	-1	1
34	Modern consensus, 2nd c.	Almost Certain	-1	1
35	Daniel in Hagiographa	Almost Certain	-1	1
36	Daniel 9:2	Highly Likely	1	-1
37	Babylon v. Persian law	Almost Certain	1	-1
38	Recovery of Belshazzar's name	Almost Certain	1	-1
39	Nebuchadnezzar and Jews	Almost Certain	1	-1
40	Encourage Jews, 2nd c.	Very Unlikely	1	-1
41	Ezekiel's Daniel, Ugaritic	Very Unlikely	1	-1
42	Porphyry Daniel 2nd c.	Almost Certain	-1	1
43	Vaticinium ex eventu	Highly Likely	-1	1
44	Daniel wisdom in Ezekiel	Highly Likely	1	-1

APPENDIX A: ANALYSIS OF COMPETING HYPOTHESES

Summary: There are forty-four lines of evidence. The following summarizes the confirming and disconfirming evidence:

Lines of evidence	H_1	H_2
Confirming	36	5
Disconfirming	5	36

Lines of Evidence Explained:

1. The book of Daniel was written in Hebrew (chs. 1–2a; 8–12) and Aramaic (chs. 2b–7).
2. The Aramaic chapters were written for everyone, including gentiles.
3. The Hebrew portion of the book was written for Jews. Daniel 12:9 reads, "The words are rolled up and sealed." Sealing up the words means preserving them for when they will be needed later in history.[2]
4. Aramaic portions are similar to the fifth century BC Elephantine papyri.[3]
5. Aramaic written in imperial (i.e., non-Palestinian) style.[4]
6. Three Greek words were borrowed for musical instruments, an argument for a second century author; however, Greeks had influenced and had been present in Mesopotamia since 800 BC.[5]
7. There are no Greek words for government, though Palestine would have been hellenized for 160 years before a second century author would have written.
8. Fifteen Persian words were borrowed by Daniel for government and administration, consistent with a late sixth century author.[6]
9. Daniel first mentioned Belshazzar before modern archaeology knew of him. A second century author would have yet to learn of him.[7] See E11 below.

---

2. Ice, "Running," 2.
3. Archer, *Survey*, 397.
4. Archer, *Survey*, 397; Haughwot, *Dating Daniel*, 4–5.
5. Archer, *Survey*, 395–96; Yamauchi, "Daniel and Contacts," 37–47.
6. Archer, *Survey*, 397; Conklin, "Evidences," 19.
7. Archer, *Survey*, 391.

APPENDIX A: ANALYSIS OF COMPETING HYPOTHESES

10. Due to Xerxes's destruction, Babylon was lost to history fifty years after its fall.[8]

11. Herodotus (ca. 450 BC) did not record Belshazzar's name, though he visited the ruins of Babylon in 447 BC, indicating that Babylonian history was lost.[9]

12. Daniel knew Nabopolassar, Nebuchadnezzar's father, was the son of a lowly man (Dan 4:17); "Nabo" means "in my littleness."[10]

13. Daniel's accurate description of Babylonian and Persian court life would have been unavailable to an author in the second century BC. See E10 and E11 above.

14. Daniel's description of Babylonian and Persian succession would have been unavailable for an author in the second century BC. See E10 and E11 above.

15. Daniel's description of Mesopotamian geography would have been less available for an author in the second century BC.

16. Daniel's description of the Babylonian/Persian pantheon/religion would have been less available for an author in the second century BC.

17. The book of Daniel has a solid overall narrative coherence. See E18 above.

18. Daniel used a chiastic structure to link the narrative and apocalyptic parts of the book.[11]

19. Daniel's near contemporary, the prophet Ezekiel, cites Daniel as wise and righteous in Ezek 14:14–20 and 29:3.[12]

20. Second century Qumran scrolls include all of the book of Daniel. It was too close to the time of Antiochus Epiphanes IV for Jews to consider the book of Daniel as inspired and canonical, as argued by the second century authorship theory.[13]

---

8. Conklin, "Evidences," 4.
9. Archer, *Survey*, 391–392; Conklin, "Evidences," 8.
10. Bryce, *Babylonia*, 72; McDowell, *Critics' Den*, 12–13.
11. Edlin, *Daniel*, 32; Widder, "Heart and Hope," 31–32.
12. Edlin, *Daniel*, 29.
13. Haughwot, *Dating Daniel*, 12.

APPENDIX A: ANALYSIS OF COMPETING HYPOTHESES

21. None of the sectarian documents at Qumran are similar to Daniel's use of Hebrew, indicating an earlier time for his book.[14]
22. The canonicity of the book of Daniel was affirmed by the Jews, maybe as early as the second century.[15]
23. Jews would have affirmed Daniel as a prophet by the internal test of prophecy (Deut 18:22).[16]
24. Jesus refers to Daniel as a person, not a book, by the Greek use of the preposition *dia*.[17]
25. Jesus cites sections of the book of Daniel, including the Aramaic portion (Dan 3 in Matt 13:42, 50), the contested chapter (Dan 7 in Matt 24:30; Mark 13:26, 14:62), and the Hebrew portion with Dan 9 (Matt 24:15) and Dan 11 (Mark 13:14).
26. The apostles Paul (1 Thess 4–5; 2 Thess. 2; 1 Cor 15) and John (Revelation) use Daniel's prophecies.[18]
27. Early church fathers affirmed the canonicity of the book of Daniel.[19]
28. Josephus, writing in the first century AD, says that Jaddua the high priest presented the book of Daniel to Alexander the Great when he arrived in Jerusalem in 332 BC.[20]
29. Critics argue that Dan 11:36–40 becomes historically confused. Conservative scholars believe it begins to refer to a then-future version of Antiochus Epiphanes, of which he is a type. A type is an unspoken prophecy used throughout the Scriptures.[21]
30. Daniel predicted the Roman conquest of Palestine in 63 BC, which was virtually impossible for an author of the second century to anticipate.[22]

---

14. Archer, *Survey*, 400.
15. Leiman, *Canonization*, 37.
16. Archer, *Survey*, 408.
17. Archer, *Survey*, 408.
18. Edlin, *Daniel*, 20.
19. Leiman, *Canonization*, 31–50.
20. Gaebelein, *Prophet Daniel*; see also Josephus, *Antiquities*, 368.
21. Archer, *Survey*, 404.
22. Archer, *Survey*, 407.

APPENDIX A: ANALYSIS OF COMPETING HYPOTHESES

31. The second century author-date for Daniel fails to explain his prediction of the temple's destruction in AD 70. Antiochus Epiphanes defiled the temple but did not destroy it.[23]

32. Second century advocates argue, to no avail, that the madness of Antiochus Epiphanes was comparable to Nebuchadnezzar.[24]

33. Daniel's name has not been found in extra-biblical sources. However, Babylon was lost to history until the nineteenth century. The excavation of Babylon was delayed by the Iran-Iraq War, the Gulf War and Iraq War of 2003, and the looting that occurred. Much of Babylon may remain undiscovered because of an unfortunate posting of a US mechanized regiment after the 2003 invasion of Iraq on the grounds where Babylon existed.[25]

34. A modern, scholarly consensus dates the book of Daniel to the second century. But see E37 above.

35. Critics argue that Daniel is not a genuine prophecy book, as it is placed in the Hagiographa, with the prophetic books. However, see E36 below.

36. Daniel 9:2 likely refers to an already fixed prophetic canon.[26] Even so, Josephus, the LXX, and the Talmud indicate Jewish scholars considered the prophetic canon and the Hagiographa equal.

37. A second century author would not have known that Babylonian kings could enact or change mandates, whereas the laws of the Medes and Persians could not be revoked (Dan 6:8–9; Esth 1:9, 8:8).

38. Belshazzar's name was rediscovered after discovering the *Nabonidus Chronicles* in the nineteenth century. For this reason, Belshazzar, as co-regent with his father, could only offer Daniel the third position in the empire for interpreting the handwriting on the wall (Dan 5:16). Until this discovery, critics argued the book of Daniel was historically inaccurate.

---

23. Haughwot, "Dating," 19.
24. Haughwot, "Dating," 35.
25. McCarthy and Kennedy, "Babylon Wrecked." See also Curtis, "Archeologists," 2–19.
26. Leiman, *Canonization*, 26, 33.

APPENDIX A: ANALYSIS OF COMPETING HYPOTHESES

39. Nebuchadnezzar was depicted as favoring the Jews (Dan 2–4), unlike how contemporary Jews depicted Antiochus Epiphanes in the second century.[27]

40. Second century advocates argue Daniel wrote to encourage the Jews during the reign of Antiochus Epiphanes.[28]

41. Second century advocates say that Ezekiel was referring to a different person, a Dnil, in Ugaritic mythology.[29] But this Dnil was not known for piety or wisdom, the two things Daniel's contemporary in Babylon, Ezekiel, portrays of Daniel.

42. Porphyry (ca. AD 234–305) dismissed Daniel as an author's work in the second century BC, the earliest known example of this idea. However, Porphyry was a known anti-Christian Neoplatonist, and all we know of him is from Christians who opposed his argument.[30]

43. Second century advocates argue that all prophecy was *vaticinium ex eventu*, which means that the prophetic parts of Daniel were written after the fact.

44. Daniel's ability to reveal mysteries was recorded by Ezekiel in Ezek 28:3, contrary to E41 above.

---

27. Archer, *Survey*, 410, citing Gustav Hoelscher's *Die Entstehung des Buches Daniel* (1919).
28. Callahan, *Prophecy*, 164, 177.
29. Callahan, *Prophecy*, 150.
30. Jerome, *Commentary on Daniel*.

Appendix B:
Key Assumptions Check

EVERYONE EMPLOYS ASSUMPTIONS WHEN analyzing data. Assumptions influence how data is interpreted, especially when that data is ambiguous, incomplete, or contradictory. This remains true both for current intelligence analysis and for historical records. As we noted earlier in the book, we frequently need to be made aware of the assumptions we use when analyzing data and making sense of the evidence we have. For this reason, intelligence analysts will engage in another Structured Analytic Technique (SAT), known as a Key Assumptions Check.[1] A Key Assumptions Check is one of the most frequently used techniques that help analysts make explicit assumptions or preconceptions that may interfere with or adversely influence their reasoning on an intelligence issue.

While a Key Assumptions Check is essential for analyzing contemporary events or anticipating future ones, it is no less critical for the record of the past. Simple scholarly "consensus" may mainly reflect the shared underlying assumptions of those scholars. The assumptions will not change until a new paradigm emerges for scholars to agree on. This is important because crucial assumptions may be critical vulnerabilities to the analysis; that is to say, if the assumptions are wrong or misleading, then the study will be skewed. If analysts fail to understand their underlying assumptions, they will likely only look for evidence that confirms their initial hypothesis and ignore or downplay discrepant or contradictory data. Understanding the critical assumptions of the differing hypotheses will help us analyze what drives the interpretation.

For interpreting the book of Daniel, there are two dominant hypotheses regarding its authorship. The traditional and historical understanding from

---

1. Heuer and Pherson, *Structured Techniques*, 209–14.

APPENDIX B: KEY ASSUMPTIONS CHECK

before the time of Jesus Christ is that the book of Daniel was written by a single author living in the late sixth century BC. The more recent hypothesis, developed mainly since the Enlightenment, is that the book of Daniel was likely written by an anonymous Jew living during the second century BC. We only have the record of one person, a known anti-Christian in the third century AD, who held to this view before the time of the Enlightenment. Opponents claim that the remarkable prophecies or revelations of the book of Daniel are said not to have been prophetic. Instead, they are what they would call *vaticinium ex eventu* (prophecy after the fact).[2] This, of course, begs the question, why anyone would argue for this view unless they held to an assumption that either God does not exist, or that prophecy is impossible, or perhaps God exists, but people willingly lie about their record of prophecies.

The traditional and historical view of the authorship of the book of Daniel holds different assumptions. Most Jewish and Christian scholars believe in a transcendent God who created space and time; therefore, God could give prophecies or apocalypses to human authors. God exists, and thus, prophecy is possible. Many Christians also hold to the view that the Bible is inerrant, which is to say, accurate in recording what God has given human authors to tell.[3] However, that will not be included in this analysis, per se.

Each of the two hypotheses concerning the book of Daniel has two or more assumptions that may influence how they interpret data to support their hypothesis. Unfortunately, advocates sometimes fail to state those assumptions, particularly the advocates for the second century authorship hypothesis. Either they are unaware of their assumptions or unwilling to share them. The assumptions should be made explicit to determine how strongly they influence the interpretation. So, part of the process for uncovering key assumptions should occur early in the analysis and be revised repeatedly to ensure the analysis leans towards the best or most reasonable interpretation.

For the two hypotheses concerning the authorship of the book of Daniel, we may label them with A1–5 below, equaling the assumptions for each hypothesis. There may be more assumptions than I've listed here. As mentioned above, these assumptions are frequently left unstated, particularly by the advocates for the late, second-century authorship hypothesis. However, given what we have, the assumptions of these two positions are mutually exclusive. Thus, without analyzing the data, we are left with different assumptions that cancel one another out. In our analysis of the ACH,

2. Wikipedia, "Vaticinium ex eventu."
3. See, for example, Ross, *Rescuing*.

APPENDIX B: KEY ASSUMPTIONS CHECK

however, we see that the most vital element driving the interpretation of H_2 (second-century hypothesis) is its hidden assumptions. Data and evidence drive H_1.

Table 13: Key Assumptions Check			
Assumption #	Key Assumptions	H_1	H_2
A1	There is no God	-1	1
A2	Prophecy is impossible	-1	1
A3	There may be a God, but people lie	-1	1
A4	There is a God who transcends space/time	1	-1
A5	Prophecy is possible	1	-1

There are only five confirming items of evidence for H_2 and thirty-six disconfirming items. On the other hand, the traditional, historical view of the book of Daniel (H_1) argues a single, sixth-century author wrote it. This view has thirty-six lines of confirming evidence and only five disconfirming items. The strongest indicator that the assumptions of the advocates for H_2 drive the interpretation is that more evidence disconfirms it, and fewer lines of evidence support it.

The advocates of H_2 likely rely more upon the assumptions of the consensus of modern, post-Enlightenment naturalism than the evidence for the authorship of the book of Daniel. This may help explain two other things about the arguments of those who hold to this perspective. First, they may state as fact that an anonymous Jew in the second century BC wrote the book of Daniel and his prophecies were *vaticinium ex eventu*. Or, the author may defend the second-century authorship hypothesis view by distorting or downplaying the evidence for a sixth-century-BC authorship. Without going into too much detail, there have been multiple discrepant versions of the second-century-authorship hypothesis, which may only indicate some of these advocates understand its underlying problems.[4]

---

4. According to one author, the prophecy of Dan 10–12 was given to Daniel in the fifth century BC but not written down until the second century, "as established according to scholarship going back to Porphyry in the 3rd century C.E." See Scolnic, "Ptolemaic?," 158. For another author, Daniel's depiction of Antiochus IV Epiphanes takes its view from a Persian king. See Niskanen, "Daniel's Portrait," 378–86.

Appendix C: Intelligence Failure

INTELLIGENCE CAN FAIL, so intelligence agencies always look for ways to improve their analysis. Pearl Harbor and the 9/11 terror attacks are two familiar examples of intelligence analysis failing to anticipate a surprise attack. But predicting what a country or a terrorist organization is going to do is a much bigger problem of intelligence itself: this is the ability to detect and know with a high degree of certainty that something specific may happen; individuals and institutions can change their intentions much more quickly and covertly than their capabilities.

A more instructive example, however, is the failure of almost every country's intelligence agency to assess that Saddam Hussein had given up his nuclear weapons program.[1] Intelligence analysts and policymakers around the world believed Saddam had no nuclear weapons program before the Gulf War in 1991. To their surprise, after the war concluded, they learned that he had maintained a very robust and active program, and many states began enforcing inspections on his regime to ensure he would dismantle it. However, at his direction, his government performed various denial and deception activities to hide the true breadth and scope of the program. At some point, Saddam decided to dismantle the program but kept this a secret from all but a few of his closest confidants for fear of encouraging Iran to take advantage of this dismantling after Iraq had lost the Gulf War.

Because of his prior successful deception and its discovery, many analysts and policymakers hardened their view of Saddam's regime. Analysts, in particular, began to look only for evidence that confirmed their assumption that he was still engaged in nuclear weapons research and development. All

---

1. This summary and analysis is adapted from Robert Jervis, *Why Intelligence Fails*, 123–55.

new evidence that came forward was interpreted in light of this belief. Even ambiguous evidence—for example, dual-use aluminum tubes that could be used for the nuclear program or for nonnuclear purposes, was interpreted in light of this idea, which became a hard consensus.

Had the analysts at the intelligence agencies offered one more assumption to test against the evidence, they might have come to a different conclusion. The use of the Analysis of Competing Hypotheses and a Key Assumptions Check, while not a guarantee of success, may have reduced their certainty over Iraq's nuclear weapons program.

Bibliography

Ahn, John J. *Exile as Forced Migrations: A Sociological, Literary, and Theological Approach on the Displacement and Resettlement of the Southern Kingdom of Judah.* Berlin: De Gruyter, 2010. https://ebookcentral.proquest.com/lib/csusb/detail.action?docID=669171.

Alcock, Susan E., et al., eds. *Empires: Perspectives from Archaeology and History.* Cambridge: Cambridge University Press, 2001.

Archer, Gleason L., Jr. *Encyclopedia of Bible Difficulties.* Grand Rapids: Zondervan, 1982.

———. *A Survey of Old Testament: Introduction.* Rev. ed. Chicago: Moody, 1985.

Barker, Kenneth, et al., eds. *The NIV Study Bible.* Grand Rapids: Zondervan, 1985.

Barry, Phillips. "Antiochus IV, Epiphanes." *Journal of Biblical Literature* 29.2 (1910) 126–38.

Beckwith, Roger T. "Daniel 9 and the Date of Messiah's Coming in Essene, Hellenistic, Pharisaic, Zealot and Early Christian Computation." *Revue de Qumran* 10 (Dec. 1981) 521–42.

Berry, Elliot M., et al. "The Middle Eastern and Biblical Origins of the Mediterranean Diet." *Public Health Nutrition* 14 (2011–12) 2288–95.

Best, Richard A., Jr. "Intelligence Information: Need-to-Know vs. Need-to-Share." Congressional Research Service, June 6, 2011. https://sgp.fas.org/crs/intel/R41848.pdf.

Bible.org. "Who Is Ezekiel's Daniel?" https://bible.org/article/who-ezekiels-daniel.

Block, Daniel. "Is Trump Our Cyrus? The Old Testament Case for Yes and No." *Christianity Today*, Oct. 28, 2018. https://www.christianitytoday.com/ct/2018/october-web-only/donald-trump-cyrus-prophecy-old-testament.html.

Bowden, Hugh. *Alexander the Great: A Very Short Introduction.* Oxford: Oxford University Press, 2014.

Bruce, F. F. *Israel and the Nations: The History of Israel from the Exodus to the Fall of the Second Temple*, revised by David F. Payne. Downers Grove, IL: InterVarsity, 1997.

Bryce, Trevor. *Babylonia: A Very Short Introduction.* Oxford: Oxford University Press, 2016.

Callahan, Tim. *Bible Prophecy: Failure or Fulfillment?* Altadena, CA: Millennium, 1997.

Collins, John J., and Adela Yarbro Collins. *Daniel: A Commentary on the Book of Daniel.* Minneapolis: Fortress, 1993.

Conklin, David. "Evidences Relating to the Date of the Book of Daniel." https://www.666man.net/Dating_the_Book_of_Daniel_by_David_Conklin.html.

Curtis, J. "Relations Between Archeologists and the Military in the Case of Iraq." *Papers from the Institute of Archeology* 19 (2009) 2–19.

Defense Language Institute. "Language Proficiency Assessment." Foreign Language Center. https://www.dliflc.edu/academics/testing/.

BIBLIOGRAPHY

Day, John. "The Daniel of Ugarit and Ezekiel and the Hero of the Book of Daniel." *Vetus Testamentum* 30 (Apr. 1980) 174–84.

Dressler, Harold H. P. "The Identification of the Ugaritic Dnil with the Daniel of Ezekiel." *Vetus Testamentum* 29 (Apr. 1979) 152–61.

Duignan, Brian. "Postmodernism." *Encyclopedia Britannica*, Mar. 5, 2020. https://www.britannica.com/topic/postmodernism-philosophy.

Durant, Will. *The Story of Civilization: Our Oriental Heritage*. Vol. 1. New York: Simon & Schuster, 1954.

Edlin, Jim. *Daniel: A Commentary in the Wesleyan Tradition*. Kansas City: Beacon Hill, 2009.

EMDR Institute. "History of EMDR Therapy." https://www.emdr.com/history-of-emdr/.

ESV Study Bible. Wheaton, IL: Crossway, 2008.

Fewell, Danna. *Circle of Sovereignty: A Story of Stories in Daniel 1–6*. N.p.: Almond, 1988.

The Foundation for Critical Thinking. "Distinguishing Between Inferences and Assumptions." https://www.criticalthinking.org/pages/distinguishing-between-inferences-and-assumptions/484.

Gaebelein, Arno C. *The Prophet Daniel: A Key to the Visions and Prophecies of the Book of Daniel*. New York: Our Hope, 1911. Kindle.

Gentry, Peter J. "Daniel's Seventy Weeks and the New Exodus." *Southern Baptist Journal of Theology* 14.1 (2010) 26–44.

Gerig, Bruce L. "Eunuchs in the OT, Part 1: Introduction and Summary." *Epistle*, Last updated 2010. http://epistle.us/hbarticles/eunuchs1.html.

Harris, R. Laird, et al. *Theological Workbook of the Old Testament*. Vol. 2. Chicago: Moody, 1980.

Haughwot, Mark S. *Dating the Book of Daniel: A Survey of the Evidence for an Early Date*. Last updated June 3, 2024. https://markhaughwout.com/Bible/Dating_Daniel.pdf.

Heiser, Michael. *The Unseen Realm: Recovering the Supernatural Worldview of the Bible*. Bellingham, WA: Lexham, 2015.

Heuer, Richards J., Jr. *Psychology of Intelligence Analysis*. N.p.: Center for the Study of Intelligence, 1999.

Heuer, Richards J., Jr., and Randolph H. Pherson. *Structured Analytic Techniques for Intelligence Analysis*. Washington, DC: CQ, 2011.

Hodges, Chris. *The Daniel Dilemma: How to Stand Firm and Love Well in a Compromise Culture*. Nashville: Nelson, 2017.

Hood, Marilynn E. *Daniel: Esteemed by God*. Hendersonville, NC: Gypsy Heart, 2017.

Ice, Thomas D. "Running To and Fro." *Article Archives* 31 (May 2009) 1–6. https://digitalcommons.liberty.edu/pretrib_arch/31/.

Jackson, Peter. *The Lord of the Rings: The Fellowship of the Ring*. Burbank, CA: New Line Cinema, 2001.

Jerome. *Jerome's Commentary on Daniel*. Translated by Gleason L. Archer. Eugene, OR: Wipf & Stock, 2009.

Jervis, Robert. *Perception and Misperception in International Politics*. Princeton: Princeton University Press, 1979.

———. *Why Intelligence Fails: Lessons from the Iranian Revolution and the Iraq War*. Ithaca, NY: Cornell University Press, 2010.

Josephus, *The Antiquities of the Jews*. Translated by William Whiston. Nashville: Thomas Nelson, 1998.

BIBLIOGRAPHY

———. *History of the Jews*. Translated by William Whiston. Edited by Alex Murray. London: Virtue, Spalding, 1874.

Joshua Project. "What Is the 10/40 Window?" https://joshuaproject.net/resources/articles/10_40_window.

Kelman, Herbert C. "Compliance, Identification, and Internalization: Three Processes of Attitude Change." *Journal of Conflict Resolution* 2 (Mar. 1958) 51–60.

Kuhurt, Ameilie. "The Achaemenid Persian Empire (c. 550–c. 330 BCE): Continuities, Adaptation, Transformation." In *Empires: Perspectives from Archaeology and History*, edited by Susan Alcock, et al., 93–123. Cambridge: Cambridge University Press, 2001.

Kriwaczek, Paul. *Babylon: Mesopotamia and the Birth of Civilization*. New York: St. Martin's, 2010.

Leiman, Sid Z. *The Canonization of Hebrew Scripture*. 2nd ed. New Haven: Connecticut Academy of Arts and Sciences, 1991.

McCarthy, Rory, and Maer Kennedy. "Babylon Wrecked by War." *Guardian*, Jan. 15, 2005.

McDowell, Josh. *Daniel in the Critics' Den*. San Bernadino, CA: Campus Crusade for Christ, 1979.

Moore, Beth. *Daniel: Lives of Integrity, Words of Prophecy*. Nashville: LifeWay, 2006.

Moscati, Sabatino. *The Face of the Ancient Orient: Near Eastern Civilization in Pre-Classical Times*. Mineola, NY: Dover, 2001.

Newsom, Carol A. *Daniel: A Commentary*. Louisville: Westminster John Knox, 2014.

Niskanen, Paul. "Daniel's Portrait of Antiochus IV: Echoes of a Persian King." *Catholic Biblical Quarterly* 66 (2004) 378–86.

Oates, Joan. *Babylon*. Rev. ed. London: Thames & Hudson, 1986.

Office of the Director of National Intelligence. *Intelligence Community Directive 203: Technical Ammendment*. Jan. 2, 2015. https://www.dni.gov/files/documents/ICD/ICD-203.pdf.

Pasupathi, Monisha. "Age Differences in Response to Conformity Pressure for Emotional and Nonemotional Material." *Psychology and Aging* 14 (1999) 170–74.

Pierce, Ronald W. "Spiritual Failure, Postponement, and Daniel 9." *Trinity Journal* 10.2 (Fall 1989) 211–22.

Rabinovich, Abraham. "Info Gathered on the Exiled." *Jerusalem Post*, July 16, 2009. https://www.jpost.com/Magazine/Features/Info-gathering-on-the-exiled.

Rana, Fazale. "Epigenetics—Sins of the Father." Reasons to Believe, June 1, 2011. https://www.reasons.org/explore/blogs/todays-new-reason-to-believe/read/tnrtb/2011/06/01/epigenetics-sins-of-the-father.

Ross, Hugh. *Why the Universe Is the Way It Is: Reasons to Believe*. Grand Rapids: Baker, 2008.

———. *Rescuing Interrancy: A Scientific Defense*. Covina, CA: RTB, 2023.

Ross, Hugh, and Kathy Ross. *Always be Ready: A Call to Adventurous Faith*. Covina, CA: RTB Press, 2018.

Schiffman, Lawrence H. "Hellenism and Judaism: Palestine Goes Greek." *My Jewish Learning*. https:www.myjewishlearning.com/article/Hellenism-judaism/.

Scolnic, Benjamin. "Is Daniel 11:1–19 Based on a Ptolemaic Narrative?" *Journal for the Study of Judaism in the Persian, Hellenistic, and Roman Period* 45 (2014) 157–84.

Seymour, Michael. *Babylon: Legend, History and the Ancient City*. London: I.B. Tauris, 2016.

Shapiro, Francine. *EMDR: The Breakthrough Eye Movement Therapy for Overcoming Anxiety, Stress, and Trauma*. New York: Basic, 2004.

Siegel, Daniel J. *Brainstorm: The Power and the Purpose of the Teenage Brain*. New York: Tarcher/Penguin, 2013.
Southwood, Katherine. Review of *Exile as Forced Migrations*, by John Ahn. *Journal of Theological Studies* 62 (Apr. 2011) 277–81.
Taagepera, Rein. "Size and Duration of Empires: Growth-Decline Curves, 3000 to 600 B.C." *Social Science Research* 7.2 (1978) 186–96.
———. "Size and Duration of Empires: Growth-Decline Curves, 600 B.C. to 600 A.D." *Social Science History* 3.3–4 (1979) 115–38.
Tacitus. *The Histories*. Translated by Kenneth Wellesley. Middlesex, UK: Penguin, 1964.
Tanner, J. Paul. "The Literary Structure of the Book of Daniel." *Bibliotheca Sacra* 160 (2003) 269–82.
Tecuci, Gheorghe, et al. *Intelligence Analysis as Discovery of Evidence, Hypotheses, and Arguments: Connecting the Dots*. New York: Cambridge University Press, 2016.
Telhami, Shibley. *Power and Leadership in International Bargaining: The Path to the Camp David Accords*. New York: Columbia University Press, 1990.
Thucydides. *The Peloponnesian War*. The Crawley Translation. Rev. ed. New York: Modern Library, 1982.
Tinder, Glenn. *The Political Meaning of Christianity: The Prophetic Stance*. Baton Rouge: Louisiana State University Press, 1989.
Turchin, Peter, et al. "East-West Orientation of Historical Empires and Modern States." *Journal of World-Systems Research* 12 (2006) 219–29.
van der Kolk, Bessel A. *The Body Keeps the Score: Brain, Mind, and Body in the Healing of Trauma*. New York: Viking, 2014.
Waltke, Bruce K. "The Textual Criticism of the Old Testament." In *Expositor's Bible Commentary*, edited by Frank E. Gaebelein, 1:209–28. Grand Rapids: Zondervan, 1979.
Walton, John H., and D. Brent Sandy. *The Lost World of Scripture: Ancient Literary Culture and Biblical Authority*. Downers Grove, IL: IVP Academic, 2013.
Waters, Matt. *Ancient Persia: A Concise History of the Achaemenid Empire, 550–330 BCE*. New York: Cambridge University Press, 2014.
Weitzman, Steven. "Plotting Antiochus's Persecution." *Journal of Biblical Literature* 123 (2004) 219–34.
Wikipedia. "Leon Trotsky." Last updated Nov. 6, 2024. https://en.wikiquote.org/wiki/Leon_Trotsky.
———. "Susa." Last updated Dec. 25, 2024. https://en.wikipedia.org/wiki/Susa.
———. "Vaticinium ex eventu." Last updated June 10, 2024. https://en.wikipedia.org/wiki/Vaticinium_ex_eventu.
Widder, Wendy. "The Heart and Hope of Daniel: Finding Connections Between the Stories and Visions." *Bible Study Magazine*, Jan./Feb. 2018.
Wiseman, D. J. "Some Historical Problems in the Book of Daniel." In *Notes on Some Problems in the Book of Daniel*, edited by D. J. Wiseman et al., 9–18. London: Tyndale, 1965.
World Health Organization (WHO). "Female Genital Mutilation." Feb. 5, 2024. https://www.who.int/news-room/fact-sheets/detail/female-genital-mutilation.
Yamauchi, Edwin. "Daniel and Contacts Between the Aegean and the Near East Before Alexander." *Evangelical Quarterly* 53 (1981) 37–47.

Index

Abductive reasoning, 3, 7, 12, 15–16
Abomination of Desolation, 138
Alexander (the Great), 73, 110, 130, 134, 136
Analysis of Competing Hypotheses, 12–15, 17, 125–27, 139–141, 152
Ancient of Days, 110
Angels, 17, 31, 88, 115–16
Anointed One, 107–108, 111–12, 118
Antichrist, 111, 114, 132, 138
Antiochus IV (Epiphanes), 7, 111–14, 118, 124–25, 128, 134, 136–38, 145–47
Apocalypse, 1, 8, 71, 109, 122, 124–25, 130, 136, 149
Aramaic, 14, 52–53, 60, 68, 106, 109, 126, 132–33, 141, 143, 145
Archer, Gleason, 94
Arioch, 61, 64–69, 83, 133
Ashpenaz, 42–43, 46, 48–50, 54–55, 64, 66, 68, 83
Assyria, 19, 42, 62–63

Babylon, 3, 16, 19–21, 27–29, 37–39, 42–45, 58, 62–63, 72–74, 76, 89–90, 92, 109–110, 117, 124, 132, 135, 141
    Astronomy, 50, 54
    Religious beliefs, 28, 44, 50–54, 59, 67
    Science, 53
    Socialization, 45–46
Belshazzar, 43, 61, 76–78, 92, 101, 110, 118, 135–36, 141–44, 146

Belteshazzar, 3, 43, 61
BLUF (Bottom line up front), 15–16

Callahan, Tim, xi–xii
Canonization, 2, 110, 128–131, 142, 146
Celestial Beings, 100, 103, 110, 112–13, 115–122
    Gabriel, 106–107, 100, 106–107, 111–13, 119, 133
    Man dressed in linen, 112–13, 117, 120–23
    Michael, 115–116
Chaldean, 17, 53–54, 59
Chiasm, 131–32, 142, 144
Cognitive Psychological Model, 11
Cosmic Spiritual Geography, 116
Cyaxeres, 62–63
Cyrus, 33–34, 46, 58, 63, 71, 78–81, 83–84, 93–94, 103, 105–106, 111

Daniel
    Diet, 56–57, 118
    Dreams/visions, 82, 112–13, 118–19, 131, 138
    Persecution of his faith, 87
    Prayer of repentance and restoration, 17, 39, 82, 96–100, 111, 119
Darius the Mede, 17, 74, 76, 79–81, 83, 86, 88–90, 92, 94, 96, 111, 115, 119, 133, 135
Dead Sea Scrolls (see Qumran)
Dietary Laws (see Levitical Laws)
Divine Council, 110, 119
D'nil (of Ugaritic Myth), 127–28, 147

INDEX

Dominion Mandate, 4
Durant, Will, 50

Egypt, 19-20, 34, 37, 42, 58, 98, 113, 138
Elephantine Papyri, 134, 143
Empire size, 72
Essenes, 108, 112,
Eunuchs, 24, 26, 30, 39, 43, 49
Evil-Marodach, 77
Eye Movement Desensitization and Reprocessing (EMDR), 28
Ezekiel, 100, 127-28, 144, 147
Ezra, 93, 103

Female Genital Mutilation, 25
Fuzzy System, 13, 139

Gospel, 29, 101
Greek (Macedonian) Empire, 71-74, 107, 109-111
    Prince of, 115,
Greek words, 134-35, 141, 143
Gubaru, 80

Habakkuk, 46-47, 94
Hagiographa, 112, 129, 142, 146
Handwriting on the wall, 76, 78-79, 82, 84, 92, 146
Heiser, Michael, 116, 120-21
Hellenization, 7, 113, 134, 143
Herodotus, 62-63, 79, 135, 141, 144
Hezekiah, 20, 23-24, 29, 39
Hypothesis Confirming Bias, 12-13, 126

Imago Dei, 35
Inspiration, 2, 129-130
Intelligence
    Analysis, 8-10, 12, 15, 51, 151-52
    Failures, 14, 151-52
    International Politics, 32, 38-39, 92, 101, 115
Isaiah, 22-24, 26, 29-30, 33-34, 39, 46, 63, 83, 101, 122

Jeremiah, 22-23, 33, 46, 63, 83, 93, 95, 101, 105
Jerome, 131

Jervis, Robert, 11
Jesus
    Messiah, 37, 40, 108, 111-12, 116, 120-21, 126-127, 132, 138
    On Daniel, 109, 130, 145
Jews, persecution, 111, 113-14, 124, 132, 137
Josephus, 130, 145
Josiah, 62
Judah, 19-20, 27, 29, 33, 37, 61, 89, 94-96, 103-106, 113, 123

Key Assumptions Check, 12, 125-26, 139-140, 148-150, 152
King of the North, 113-14
King of the South, 113-14
Kingdom of God, 4, 6, 16-17, 30-32, 35, 40-41, 52, 55, 67, 71, 74, 92, 108-109, 118, 123, 138

Language Training, 53
Letter to the Exiles, 47
Levitical Laws, 44-45, 95, 99
Limbic system, 69
Little Horn(s), 111, 114, 118, 138

Maccabean Hypothesis, 125
Magi, 63
Marduk, 43, 77, 84
Medes, 62-63, 78-79, 80-81, 90
Media, 78
Median Wall, 63
Mishnah, 129
Moon god Sin, 77, 84
Mosaic
    Messianic, 120-21
    Prophetic, 121-23, 138

Nabonassa, 53
Nabonidus, 76-77, 84, 136
    Chronicles, 146
Nabopolassar, 58-59, 62, 77-78, 136, 141, 144
Natural law, 9, 35-36
Naturalism, 2, 9
Nebuchadnezzar, 8, 20, 32-33, 46-47, 58-60, 66-71, 75-78, 82, 89, 93,

INDEX

100–101, 107, 109, 118–19, 131, 135–37, 142, 144, 146
Building campaign, 53
Dreams, 47, 59–60, 71–75, 77, 82, 100–101, 109–110, 118, 131
Need to know, 122
Neriglissar, 77
Neuroscience, 25, 54, 69
Northern Kingdom of Israel, 19

Passover, 99
Paul, Apostle, 31, 33, 51, 90, 102–103, 142, 145
Persia, 19, 71–74, 78–79, 83–84, 90, 92, 107, 109–111, 124, 132, 135
   Prince of, 115
Propaganda, 84
Pharisees, 108, 112,
Political
   Anarchy, 4, 33, 56, 89
   Authority, 4, 33, 40, 50, 55–56, 64, 66, 68, 70, 86, 88–89, 105
   Conspiracy, 70, 83, 85–88, 90, 92, 118
   Prayer for, 88
   Rule(rs), 33, 75
Porphyry, 131, 142, 147
Postmodernism, 2
Post-Traumatic Stress Disorder (PTSD), 22–23, 25–28
Princes (celestial), 116
Prince of Greece, 115
Prince of Persia, 115
Prophecy (ies), 8–9, 22–23, 29, 39, 46, 63, 93–95, 105, 129, 131–32, 142, 145, 150
   False, 23, 100
Providence, 38
Ptolemaic Empire, 73, 110, 113, 137

Roman Empire, 71–74, 109–110, 138, 145
Rulers of this age, 120–21

Qumran, xi, 128, 142, 144–45

Samaria, 19
Samaritans, 19, 112
Sandy, Brent, xii,
Satan, 31
Satrap(y), 81, 83–85
Scythians, 62–63
Seleucid Empire, 44, 73, 110, 113, 125, 137
Solomon, 48, 97–99, 103
Son of Man, 110
Sons of God, 116
Sovereignty (God's), 16, 29–35, 37–40, 47, 49, 67, 83, 86–87, 90–91, 94, 100–101, 106, 122
Susa, 78

Taagapera, Rein, 72, 74
Tacitus, 102,
Talmud, 45, 129, 146
Tanakh, 125, 128–29, 131
Tiglath-Pileser III, 52, 81
Tinder, Glenn, 4
Thucydides, 4
Torah, 128
Tower of Babel, 4, 99, 101, 115
Trauma, 20–28, 39, 42, 49
Type or typology, 114, 137, 145

Van der Kolk, Bessel, 22, 25, 27
Vaticinium ex eventu, 125, 136, 142, 147, 150

Walton, John, xii
Watchers, 116
Waters, Matt, 79
Wisdom, 3, 5–6, 37, 30, 39–40, 48, 90
Wiseman, D.J., 80
World Health Organization (WHO), 25
Worldliness, 4– 5, 18

Xerxes, 135, 144

Zealots, 108, 112

www.ingramcontent.com/pod-product-compliance
Lightning Source LLC
Chambersburg PA
CBHW050815160426
43192CB00010B/1766